A TASTE FOR LIVING

Liam Hickey

A Taste for Living
TAKE-AWAY THOUGHTS FOR
THE WEEKDAYS OF THE YEAR

THE COLUMBA PRESS
DUBLIN 1992

First edition, 1992, published by
THE COLUMBA PRESS
93 The Rise, Mount Merrion, Blackrock, Co Dublin

ISBN 1 85607 006 9

Cover by Bill Bolger
Origination by The Columba Press
Printed in Ireland by
Colour Books Ltd., Dublin

Contents

Preface

'A hundred blessings a day are there for the taking,' according to the Jewish saying. A man brought his diary to hospital. As he waited anxiously, the busy nurse passing his bedside asked, 'Would you like a cup of tea?' He marked 'one' off in the diary, and said to himself, 'Ninety-nine blessings to go.'

Our world is full of stories to be told, and every story has a blessing. The stories in this book touch on the human experiences of living and loving, grieving and dying, celebrating, praying, being single, a grandparent, married, widowed, a child, a prisoner, a contemplative. They speak of crossings and journeys, raindrops, bog oak, a vandalised tree, a dog, a bird, a daffodil. I've used the gospel of the Daily Missal as a view-finder to try to spot the blessings in the stories.

A depressed man told how he sat alone on a remote railway station platform. Only a crow kept him company. Watching the antics of that crow, he was encouraged to keep on living and hoping. He said that that dumb crow did more for him than he ever did for any bird all his life.

If a crow can be a messenger of hope, maybe the words and experiences of people in this collection of *Take-Away Thoughts for the Weekdays of the Year* can give *A Taste for Living* and a reason for coping.

Liam Hickey
St Ciaran's
Dublin 15

January 1

Mary hints that the experiences of life, even the sad ones, can be treasures of God. Surprises, disappointments, pregnancies, births, visitors, family, relations, neighbours, political happenings, emigrations, the comings and goings are all in God's providence.

Mary also hints that it is in the chapel of the heart (inside us) that we learn to cope with and appreciate what is happening. We recognise the blessings in various events. Making moments in our hearts as we go on the daily round is the basic retreat. Look lovingly at the Real – a flower arrangement, flight of a bird, the humour of people. 'She treasured and pondered in her heart.'

May God bless you and keep you.
May the Lord let his face shine on you
and be gracious to you. (*New Year Prayer*)

January 2

The priest spoke about his years in Africa. He was fascinated by the quiet of the bush and the entertainment of monkeys. 'They can do all kinds of tricks,' he said. 'They are great at gymnastics. They just need one thing that is absolutely vital. They need a reliable branch for support – a solid branch to cling to for security.'

We need a solid branch – a branch that can stand up to pressures, that can take the storms of ruffling and disappointment and the piercing heat of pain, misunderstanding, let down.

The priest suggested that the story of Jesus, as told by St Luke, was a vital steady life-line for him. The Jesus story does not change with fashions or time. Jesus takes in all. He is always new and refreshing. Catechisms and fancy books may pass, but not the Jesus story.

Sadly, we are undernourished in the humanity of Jesus. Between his birth and his dying, his story is a fully human story. To know the human Jesus is to begin to know who we are, and how we are for others. To tell our children the human stories of Jesus is the best preparation for communion and life.

There stands among you the one who is coming. *Jn 1:19-28*

January 3

Christmas is a time when we feel that we are noticed. We get gifts, cards, phone calls, invitations. We feel appreciated, that we belong.

We like to be appreciated and we have the power to show appreciation. John didn't fully appreciate Jesus when he was around. I think that he is trying to make up later on, so he overwhelms us with words about Jesus. His heart has been fired by the face, touch, voice of Jesus. He wants to tell us about him and his message.

He tells us that all the people of the world are children of God. All are also sinners. Mass-going and sacraments can help us to grow in appreciation of our own God-given humanity and the humanity of others.

We are already the children of God. *Jn 2:29-3:6*

January 4

The sermon we see is always better than the sermon we hear. Give the little girl something to eat. Give the lads a mug of wine, it's a wedding day. No need for long or gloomy sermons. God Our Father celebrates.

I think that Jesus is anxious to get across that religion is not about answers or knowing laws. It is a way of living. If God is Father and I am loved in spite of my sins, that is a great start and surely good news. It is also a challenge and a joy, and it doesn't change.

Come and see. *Jn 1:35-42*

January 5

John wrote a letter to his girl friend: 'Darling, I would climb the highest mountain just to see you. I would walk the hot desert to hold your hand. I would swim all the oceans for one kiss.' At the bottom of the page he wrote: 'P.S. See you to-morrow night, if it's not raining.'

Jesus's best friend, John, says that our love must not be mere words but real and active. That is why the real test of religion is how we behave, how we relate to and treat others. John gives us the good news: God is love.

My children, our love is not to be just words or mere talk. *1 Jn 3:11-21*

January 6 Epiphany

The kings in the crib, the colourful magi at the end of their journey, tell an exciting story: God is for all people. (What colour is God's skin?) They also tell us that God hides his wonder and beauty in all kinds of ways – in babies and mothers, in rich and poor, in city and country, in palaces and huts.

We are always searchers, on a journey from birth to death. I believe that the Church is a good guide in our search, but it has no monopoly of truth. Being Church involves not only a special relationship with God, but also with the neighbour. It is communion with one another which is celebrated, in memory of Jesus, with the breaking of bread at Mass.

You have given us eternal life, and this life is in your Son.
1 Jn 5:5-13

Note to Reader:

Depending on which day of the week the Epiphany falls, pick the next day from the following pages, entitled 'after the Epiphany' and follow through until Saturday.

Monday after Epiphany

I grew up with turf cutting. Deep down the cutter would sometimes strike wood. This was a nuisance and frustrating, cutting through or around 'bog oak'. One day an artist looked long and lovingly at a stump of bog oak. As he fondled this 'piece of ordinary nuisance' he sensed a priceless treasure. He held a jewel in his hands. He followed his dream through. I went to see his Exhibition of Bog Oak Art recently in Dublin. There the wood-sculptor gave a voice to treasures that have lain hidden for five thousand years in the bog. Each piece is an original in beauty. The grained 'oakiness and colour' in different forms and design delight the mind and inspire wonder and awe.

Jesus was always inviting us to 'look again' at the ordinary experiences of life. We can see a baby's first smile, a flight of birds, a dog wagging his tail, meeting people, as kingdom of God – close at hand. Mass celebrates and illustrates all these blessings of life.

The kingdom of heaven is close at hand. *Mt 4:12-25*

Tuesday after Epiphany

Mothers often say that life for them is just endlessly preparing meals. A served meal is always appreciated by home cooks. Life and religion is lived in the getting of meals.

In the meal-time story today the Lord teaches that getting people together to eat eases loneliness and is an encouragement. But meals don't happen by just praying – effort has to be made. There has to be planning, going to shops, bags, baskets and trolleys. Planning food dishes involves a lot of practical loving. This work of 'giving them something to eat' is blessed by God. God's providence enters into the eating and drinking, the scraps and scrapes of life. Pots and pans and bills – all are the raw material of Sunday's thanks and prayer.

Give them something to eat yourselves. *Mk 6:34-44*

Wednesday after Epiphany

People crowded into the little hospital mortuary chapel. The mother held the baby in her arms, cuddling him to her face. He seemed totally alive. The nurse asked me to stay for the cradling. I waited and watched. A few times the nurse whispered gently and patiently to the mother if she would now like to place the baby in the white casket. She said, 'I'm not ready just yet.' All waited. Then, in her own time, the mother stood and carried her baby to the white casket. 'His face is warm now,' she said. Mother and nurse arranged the baby, then adjusted his wrapping clothes. Baby Jonathan was at his best.

The mother placed the white wooden top over the body. I helped fasten the screw crosses into place. There are different kind of 'presences' in standing and waiting in silence, and crowds in grief being dumbfounded.

They were utterly dumbfounded. *Mk 6:45-52*

Thursday after Epiphany

The confirmation class prepared posters for display in the Church. They were celebrating Confirmation day. It was interesting to see how they thought of the Spirit of God as involved in all of life – brooding over all creation. There were expressions of life touching mind, heart and body. There was family life, community life, the life of our environment – air and water. They prayed for awareness.

The Lord and giver of life surrounds us and embraces us. The good news is that, although we are poor in spirit, with endless limitations, yet we have a God-given capacity for love and caring. God made the world, but he didn't finish it. He has given us that privilege – to make our world a better world. Our young people carry that excitement in their hearts.

He sent me to bring good news to the poor. *Lk 4:14-22*

Friday after Epiphany

'Helping Hands' caught my eye at the exhibition, a wooden sculptor piece commissioned for a hospital. Two pairs of hands stretched out caringly and lovingly towards each other. I thought of all the hands that channel God's blessing to the sick and to all our lives. There are stretchers and ambulances, secretaries and telephonists. We have nursing, catering, medical, scientific hands. We are supported by family hands, community hands, teaching hands.

The raised hands of the priest celebrate all the ways we are touched by others and all the ways we are empowered to touch others with multiple blessings.

Jesus stretched out his hand and touched him. *Lk 5:12-16*

Saturday after Epiphany

Brídín never got over the death of her husband. She was now dying, but finding it difficult to go. Her daughter whispered to her, 'Ma, let go! Da is waiting for you. He is looking forward to meeting you.'

Letting go makes one shudder a little and very conscious of limitations. It is human to feel sad when our achievements are slipping away from us, when what we have worked so hard for seems to fade or to be forgotten and not appreciated. Leaving the business, leaving the parish, leaving the team, leaving or shedding hurts that are pad-locked into our make-up, is a mighty mission.

John the Baptist is the saint of 'letting go'. 'Your fan club has gone after Jesus, your cousin,' he was told. 'My joy is full,' he said. 'My job was to introduce, not to take the glory.' John, we really need your prayers and strength.

This same joy I feel, and now it is complete. *Jn 3:22-30*

Note to Reader:

On Monday, after the Feast of the Baptism of the Lord, turn to page 49 and use the material for the First Week in Ordinary Time. Stay with Ordinary Time until Ash Wednesday, when you turn back to page 14.

Ash Wednesday

The infants' teacher said that her little ones had a great interest in Ash Wednesday. What are the ashes? Where did they come from? Why do we bless with ashes? Can we be included in this year's Church celebrations?

The teacher's enthusiasm not only helped my tiring 'ashes faith' but also prompted me to make some ashes. We burned some small pieces of 'Palm' in the sanctuary, in full view of eight hundred and fifty pairs of eyes. We had a controlled flame to view for fifteen minutes during our celebration ceremony. All the ashes we use in the church today are made like that. The little green pieces of palm turn to ashes when burnt. They change.

We prayed:
Lord, change our hearts when we hurt others with unkind words or names. Lord, hear us.
Lord, change hearts that make violence and wars. Help us to make peace. Lord, hear us.
Lord, change the hearts of people who are well off and well fed. Help us to feed those who are hungry. Lord, hear us.
Lord, change young hearts to care for and listen to older people. Change older hearts to encourage young people. Lord,   hear us.

The burning palms gave out a sweet perfume. When someone is kind to us, it is like perfume. We try to be kind to one another during Lent. Each pupil had written out a secret promise to help someone today, at home, in school or far away. The promises were placed at the baptismal font. I really enjoyed this Ash Wednesday celebration and felt grateful to the children and to their teachers.

To add icing to the cake, I received a letter from Third Class, decorated with drawings and colours. It said: 'We were delighted and excited to see the palms burning today on the altar. We have never seen a fire in church before. We enjoyed geting the ashes on our foreheads and we will try very hard to keep our secret promises. Thank you for helping us to understand Ash Wednesday. Love from Room 3.'

Come back with all your heart ... let your hearts be broken, not your garments ... a sincere heart create for me. O God.   *Joel 2:12-18*

Thursday after Ash Wednesday

You have probably spent this morning giving life, preparing and serving food, getting ready for school, working for 'bread' as we say. People involved with the young, with football teams, community activities, nurture and promote the growth of life. How often we are made feel more alive by a word of praise or thanks, an unexpected card or phone call, a cup of tea or a visit.

Your ordinary everyday unselfishness is an extraordinary celebration of life.

Choose life – anyone who loses life for my sake will find it.

Deut 30:15-20

Friday after Ash Wednesday

The shopman said, 'There's a great trade in the doughnuts.' They did look juicy and jammy and brown. He said the children had given up sweets for Lent and switched to doughnuts.

Children are so creative and honest. They carry God's smile and message. They don't take themselves or their fast too seriously.

The Church calls Lent a joyful season. God says, 'Please don't hang your head in sadness or be quarrelsome for me. Make yourself feel good. Make a neighbour feel good. Hold your breath on harsh, begrudging words about anybody.'

Look, you quarrel and squabble when you fast, hanging your head like a reed. The fast that pleases me is to share your bread with the hungry – clothe the one you see naked. *Is 58:1-9*

Saturday after Ash Wednesday

Sister Wendy Beckett is a contemplative Nun. She says virtue is derived from the Latin word 'virtus' meaning strength, and prayer will teach us the strength to accept our weakness. It is God who prays in us, not we ourselves.

The virtuous, who felt self-sufficient and had no need of God or help, cannot hear his call. But the sinner and the sick welcomed his invitation.

It is his strength we are offered in prayer to accept our weakness.

'I have not come to call the virtuous, but the sinners to repentance.'

Lk 5:27-32

First Week of Lent: Monday

St Teresa of Avila says we cannot be sure if we love God because we cannot see him. But we can have a good idea if we love a fellow human being.

There are all kinds of hungers we can help feed. Hunger for affection is very deep in all of us. Wouldn't it be a great idea in Lent to keep an eye out for the forgotten one, the unpopular one, the child that irritates.

We show our love for God by loving the people around us.

I was hungry ... I was thirsty ... sick ... a stranger ... in prison. *Mt 25:31-46*

First Week of Lent: Tuesday

A little boy going to bed kept asking his Mam, 'Will the snow be there in the morning?' The snow was more exciting for him than his Christmas presents or Santa Claus.

Have we lost our wonder at the everyday blessings? Every snow flake is a unique masterpiece, every drop of rain is a miracle. A bird sings, a snow drop appears, a Thank You is said. All these are signs of God's constant forgiveness, lest we forget. His goodness is there before we even think or ask.

The rain and the snow come down from the heavens. *Is 55:10-11*

First Week of Lent: Wednesday

I see a little child darting across a busy street. The mother slaps the child and says, 'I'll murder you if you do that again.'

It is a language of love. The writer uses this kind of language when he talks of God's care for his people. He threatens for our good but never carries out the threat.

The people of Ninevah were killing each other. Jonah thought they were no-gooders – not worthy of God. He had to change his thinking about God, and so do we.

God saw their efforts to renounce their evil. *Jonah 3:1-10*

First Week of Lent: Thursday

Esther prayed to see life God's way and for the courage to keep going, struggling through what she could not understand.

Jesus tells us to ask the Father. We are not self-sufficient. When we light a candle or say a prayer, it is better to ask God to reveal himself rather than to tell him what to do.

Lord, let me know something of your mystery
and your way of seeing life.
Let me see your beauty and goodness.
Do what is best for me.
Lord reveal yourself. Give me courage. *Esther 4-17*

First Week of Lent: Friday

I heard a doctor say that hate, bitterness or jealousy can give you bad health, and could even accelerate a cancer or arthritis condition.

Jesus gives us the strength to throw out the killer weeds of hate, bitterness and jealousy. He even gives us the strength to make the first move: 'Go first and be reconciled with your brother...'

Repeating the Our Father slowly could be good therapy. '... as we forgive those who trespass against us.'

Go, be reconciled with your brother first. *Mt 5:20-26*

First Week of Lent: Saturday

Six young people asked for 'A Fast Pack'. They explained that their fast to-day would help someone to live.

The Lord says that fasting is a giving of life to others, not a taking of notice to oneself. So I have to beware if the whole world suffers because I give up sugar, sweets or drink. We give life to people, especially those nearest to us, everyday at home. Life is made up of cups of tea, making beds, tidying up, minding babies, meeting people.

The Pharisees got the wrong angle on fasting. Jesus says it means making another feel good, giving joy.

When you fast do not put on a gloomy look. *Mt 61:6, 16-18*

Second Week in Lent: Monday

Hearing that I should be grateful for the great gift of faith never touched my heart much as a youngster. In fact, I used to feel that it was rather a burden that stopped me from enjoying life – a kind of kill-joy obstacle.

The faith is not so much a list of things to be learned like the creed. Rather faith is a way of seeeing life – God, oneself, the neighbour, the world. Christ says it is a gift he chooses to give in his way.

This morning I watched a little child with a pack on her back going to school. She wanted to race ahead, but the mother had also to cope with the little fellow who was too weak to keep pace. So the mother took the weak one in her arms and ran after the strong one to be with her. God Our Father is like that – taking the weak in his arms, pursuing the strong with a patient love.

Your Father is compassionate. *Lk 6:36-38*

Second Week of Lent: Tuesday

God is like a father talking to his child, teaching him to appreciate life and how to make the most of it. 'Try to be honest. Play fair. Never belittle another human being. Have an eye for the weak one and the under-dog.' The constant everyday service of home-keeping is a service of love.

Come let us talk this over, God says. *Is 16-20*

Second Week of Lent: Wednesday

The struggle and pain of our everyday living sometimes leave us almost in despair. Under this kind of stress, Jesus prayed, 'Into your hands I commit my spirit.' It was a prayer of confidence – the confidence of a frightened child, jumping from the window of a burning house into the safe hands of a Father who calls his name and knows him.

Into your hands I commend my Spirit. *Ps 30*

Second Week of Lent: Thursday

A man complained to God that he had been good all his life, regular at Mass, faithful to home and family, did his job well. Things went wrong. Now he was in a bad way for money. He said to God,

'Please let me win the lottery, God. It doesn't make any difference to you and I do really deserve it and need it.' He prayed and prayed but nothing happened. Then one night he had a dream. An angel from God said 'For Christ's sake, the least you might do is to buy a lottery ticket. If you are not in, you can't win.'

The good God does not ask us to save the world. He does ask for something: to share food, to help in the street at home. And he gives us opportunities. But we can be so busy stuffing ourselves with food that we don't notice those who would thank us for the crumbs.

A poor man longed to fill himself with scraps that fell from the rich man's table. *Lk 16:19-31*

Second Week of Lent: Friday

Do you believe in dreams? There is a mystery about dreams. They are real and unreal.

Jesus says that God our Father is a dreamer about us. He is like a dream landlord. The tenants refuse to pay the rent and, instead of taking them to court, he sends his only son to plead with them.

Who would do that only a dreamer? God's love for us is a dream in its extravagance.

Here comes the man of dreams. Let's kill him. *Gen 37:12-13*

Second Week of Lent: Saturday

'Thank you God for loving me,' is the beginning of the Act of Sorrow that children say. Then later comes sorrow for my sins, 'for not loving others.'

The prayer reminds me of the story of the prodigal father who never stops loving his prodigal son. He awaits his son's return, will not allow him to confess his list of failures, but calls for celebration.

I have tried to follow that pattern of celebration in the Sacrament of Forgiveness. I was happy when someone called the celebration 'Cheap Grace'. God's grace is cheap. In fact it cannot be bought at all. It is God's extravagant love lavished on us all the time.

This man welcomes sinners and eats with them. *Lk 15:1-32*

Third Week of Lent: Monday

A song of Simon Garfunkel was 'I am a Rock, I am an island.' A rock can feel no pain and an island never cries. It is really a song of loneliness, feeling isolated, and searching for a Rock of hope. Jesus is described as a Rock that we can cling to. He has been stricken, crushed, broken. He has life-giving power.

It is often said that we have to go through suffering, pain, and failure ourselves before we can understand the pain and loneliness of others. Then we are slow to judge anyone harshly.

My soul is thirsting for God
The God of my life. *Ps 41*

Third Week of Lent: Tuesday

A prayer was found in a concentration camp where thousands of people had been starved and gassed to death. The prayer said, 'Lord may the fruits of our sufferings which made us support, care and encourage each other in pain, be collected together and (accepted) as a gift of forgiveness for those who tortured us. Look not on their evil deeds but on our blessings on their behalf.'

What makes Christianity a different religion is that it stresses the power to forgive.

Let the humbled spirit be as acceptable to you as holocausts.
Such let our sacrifice be. *Dan 3:34-43*

Third Week of Lent: Wednesday

'He sends out his word to the earth.' His word is snow – every flake different and unique. His word is ice – billions of dazzling crystals catching light. His word is the new lamb, the singing bird, nest-making, the snowdrop, the Spring smells in the air. He makes his word known to his people. His word is Jesus, the word made flesh. 'I teach you laws. Observe them that you may have life.'

He sends out his word to the earth. *Ps 147*

Third Week of Lent: Thursday

'God could not be everywhere so he made mothers.'

The missing door on the telephone box was an advantage. The mother could hold the phone with one hand, the baby's buggy with the other hand and try to pacify Kevin who was restless and teasing the baby. As I passed the mother said to the little Kevin 'don't shout at her, talk to her.' That gave me a thought for the day. Talk rather than shout. How many wounds in marriage, in business life, in relationships could be healed or soothed with talking rather than shouting. Christ was a talker not a shouter.

The dumb man spoke... People were amazed. *Lk 11: 14-23*

Third Week of Lent: Friday

I read on a greeting card, 'We must spend sometime making our own rainbow.' A little man was painting away at rainbow colours.

Loving oneself was not stressed much by family or Church in my day. The emphasis was on 'suppress thyself.' It is rightly said that unless we can love ourselves we cannot love others. But why should we love ourselves? Because we are of God and God does not make rubbish. God loves us wholeheartedly, not as perfect people, but with our warts, wounds, failings and all. God reminds us that he is 'God with us'. That is his name. All fruitfulness in life is from him.

I will fall like dew on you. All your fruitfulness comes from me. *Hosea 14:2-10*

Third Week of Lent: Saturday

I never really noticed the way rain falls. Not like out of a tap or out of a bucket. Not even like a spray. More like sheets or lines, millions and millions of drops, single drops. The drops fell on murky pools on the roadside. Each drop seemed to dance on the pool surface making all kinds of images and little bubbles that went happily on stream, and then were gone. Raindrops on the windscreen of the car made thousands of shapes, catching the jewelled light. The light went green. Time to go. God showered the world with billions of rain drops of love, to soften our hearts to give us joy.

He will come to us as showers come like Spring rains. *Hosea 5 15-66.*

Fourth Week of Lent: Monday

It is a lovely house, but not a home. What makes a home? It is the way we get on together that makes home. It is never perfect harmony. Home life depends on the way we treat each other, the way we share, the way we talk out and even give out.

Lisa gave a lovely card on Mother's Day with 'x's and hugs and love to Mam. That evening, when Mam asked help to get a meal ready, Lisa complained saying, 'I did it last time.' Mam said, 'I'm fed up with you lot. You are so selfish. I'll do it myself.' There was unhappiness at tea-time.

We have to choose ways of loving that please others, not just ourselves. That is making a house a home. Jesus talked a lot about home.

Go home. Your Son will live. *Jn 4:43-54*

Fourth Week of Lent: Tuesday

I've been to Lourdes many times. I never saw or met a miracle cure. I have met many who were healed, sick people finding strength to go on accepting and forgiving themselves; shy people getting involved with helping the sick; renewed people getting involved in parish and community work.

The miracles which get the publicity at Lourdes are the physical miracles associated with the water. But God's healing works in more ways than one.

I have no one to put me into the pool. *Jn 5:1-3*

Fourth Week of Lent: Wednesday

The young people quizzed me. 'Why does God not stop evil things happening and stop evil people harming others?' We can never fully grasp the mystery of God.

We think of God as a God of power. But God presents himself as God of love. Love does not force itself on people or things.

God is compassion and he suffers with his people. He supports everyone who falls. He opens new doors when other doors close. God is with us, rather than remote. 'I am who I am.'

My father goes on working. So do I. *Jn 5:17-30*

Fourth Week of Lent: Thursday

The teacher said, 'If the child does well at school, the parent takes the honour; if the child is weak at school, the teacher takes the blame.' We're human and funny about our blind spots.

God says, 'Moses, your people are making a mess of themselves.' Moses says 'Hold on, Lord, they are your people, and may I remind you of how good you were to our people?'

I suppose prayer is like that, reminding God of his goodness. There is a hint of great intimacy in the way Moses talks to God for the people's sake. He is prepared to beg, barter, promise, plead, negotiate, get angry. Jesus is aptly called 'The Second Moses'.

Go, your people have apostasised.
Lord, why blaze against this people of yours? *Ex 32:7-14*

Fourth Week of Lent: Friday

The Birmingham Six were wrongly imprisoned for sixteen and a half years. A priest who believed in their innocence from the beginning and campaigned for justice explained that he was insulted and rejected, threatened and abused by all kinds of people, including the media and others in power positions. Taking a stand for honesty, truth and justice brings pain.

Jesus was crucified, not for his army but for his ideas of fairness and respect for people, especially the underdogs.

Jesus went up quite privately. They said, 'Isn't this the one they want to kill?' *Mt 7:10-30*

Fourth Week of Lent: Saturday

A young tree was vandalised in the park. I found the broken limb. It was tortured and torn. 'I wanted to live,' it said, 'grow with my brothers and sisters and breathe goodness to the world. I wanted to be with the fashion of the seasons, giving delight to the young heart and maturing mind, and joy to the world.'

Later that Good Friday evening, we touched and kissed that broken tree limb. It hangs in blessing over the mantlepiece. There is death and resurrection here.

Let us destroy the tree in its strength. Let us cut him off.
Jn 11:18-20

Fifth Week of Lent: Monday

Two exciting stories today: elderly judges seducing the beautiful Suzanne and accusing her wrongly, and Jesus meeting the woman in adultery who is also accused. Tragedy seems to have won the day but, strangely, out of desperation and hopelessness come hope and forgiveness. It is God's pattern.

Our sexuality is a most God-like gift because it relates us to others and makes new life. Because it is a spark of God in our humanity, it carries joy and sadness and is an ongoing challenge. There is a hunger of the flesh, a deep longing for intimacy in every human person. The Lord seems very tolerant and understanding of this hunger; but he is strong in prompting us to share food with others.

Neither do I condemn you. *Jn 8:1-11*

Fifth Week of Lent: Tuesday

There was great joy at the celebration. They adopted a new baby. The new mother said that she was giving up her job for a year or two to be with the baby. 'It will be a difficult sacrifice,' she said, 'We'll have to miss out on things we cannot afford for the house. But time with the baby comes first. The pain will be worth it.'

The psychologist warns that a lot of teen problems arise because we don't face the reality of pain. He calls it the 'Road Less Travelled'. There isn't a pill for every inconvenience. Pain accepted and suffered for love's sake is life giving.

The Son of man lifted up ... will draw all to him. *Jn 8:21-30*

Fifth Week of Lent: Wednesday

Do you know the story of the three men in the fiery furnace? It reminded me of the words, 'Jesus descended into Hell.' Fr Rolheiser explains that Jesus enters the hell of our lives. He touches and saves by his presence. His love heals.

Depression, loneliness, break-up in marriage are often called 'hell'. Jesus has entered into hell and destroyed it. He is with us to heal and help.

Our God is able to save us.

I can see men walking about freely in the heart of the fire without any harm. *Dan 3:14-28*

Fifth Week of Lent: Thursday

An old man lay dying in a hospital bed. His face was ravaged with pain. He looked ugly. His wife at his bedside leaned across, kissed and caressed him and whispered, 'You are beautiful.' He opened his eyes and smiled.

Death happens when we cease to love – not when we cease to live. God sends out his word through millions of caring and loving hands and hearts everyday.

Who ever keeps my word will never see death. *Jn 8:51-59*

Fifth Week in Lent: Friday

John B. Keane wrote a play called *The Year of the Hiker*. It is about a family man who felt that he had to leave home and children because there was no home life, no happiness for him due to the presence of a sister-in-law in the home. She destroyed his love, so he went on the roads. He was misunderstood by his wife and children. There is great pain and sadness.

Jesus is presented as a misunderstood man. The work of his Father was that he would show God's loving heart, and untwist the false ideas that people had about God. They thought of God as punishing people or burdening them with inhuman laws. The authorities could not take Jesus's ideas. The lonely, poor and sinners were often more open to Jesus' ideas than they were.

I have done the works of my Father. You stone me. *Jn 10:31-42*

Fifth Week of Lent: Saturday

We are a scattered people, like jig-saw pieces in the making, or unfinished symphonies. God's bits and pieces, we are easily ruffled and upset. The mind and imagination can be miles away while we look into another person's eyes. It is not a nice experience when someone is shaking hands with you, but looking at and preoccupied with someone else.

Jesus made people feel special and important. He promises to gather us together. It is our job now to begin this gathering, in the everyday meetings with those at home, those on the street, people in the community, being together at Mass.

The scattered children. *Jn 11:45-57*

Holy Week: Monday

Marie Baulfer was twenty years in a Mental Home. She could not walk, talk or eat for two years. In her struggle to regain herself, to be a human being, there was a patient, Joe, who showed her a first sign of love when he bought her perfume and a scarf. Her first kiss was a miracle of new life. It started with Joe.

The story of Holy Week is about love. Reason would say that buying perfume was a waste of money, money which should be given to the poor. Love says that the poor is the one living nearest to us – maybe in riches but with a lonely heart.

Mary brought in a pound of very costly ointment ... the house was full of scent. *Jn 12:1-11*

Holy Week: Tuesday

I watched the daffodil during the storm. It bent back and forward, tossed up and down, was all shook up but held its head. The old wooden gate standing against the wall was blown down easily with a few blasts. There is a secret here for human survival. Somehow the daffodil was able to adjust, accept weakness, and onslaught. It was flexible and was well-grounded in Mother Earth. It acknowledged being dependent, not self sufficient. My poor wooden friend was stiff and stubborn and had no strong roots.

My God is my strength.
On you I have leaned from my birth. *Ps 70*

Holy Week: Wednesday

I was amused by a newspaper writer who could not find a satisfying liturgy in his own county. I wondered what he would do on Sunday, with half a church of unattached children, crying babies, distracted adults. A totally satisfying experience of liturgy can not be guaranteed, because we, who make liturgy, are so human.

'The first liturgy' in Holy Week was a mixed bag. The Psalm reflects Jesus' feelings of shame, a stranger, broken hearted. Those sitting around him at table are a mixture of betrayal, suffering and confusion. Such is the first Mass and birth of the Church – a mix of sinner and saint. We are tempted to become elitist. It is not Jesus' way.

Shame covers my face... become a stranger – Broken my heart – end of my strength – thirsty. *Ps 68*

Holy Thursday

Miss Daisy is a wealthy snob. Due to weakened health, she is no longer able to drive her car. Her son employs a driver who is black. She resents him driving her car or even touching any of her property. He is tolerant and kind. She gets hospitalised with a stroke. He is her most loyal and frequent visitor. The film closes with the black driver feeding Miss Daisy who is unable to feed herself. He gently breaks the little delicacies and, without words but with sighs of gentleness, he satisfies his patient's tastes. She says. 'You are my best friend.'

Jesus is our best friend who comes to us because we are weak, stubborn, hurtful, unkind. We are broken. He comes gently – never forces. He comes to heal us, to tell us we're special that there are depths of love and goodness in us. He encourages us to care for one another.

Jesus began to wash the disciples' feet. *Jn 13:1-15*

Good Friday

Eileen battled with the bottle in the later years. I sensed a great disappointment in her life. She was tall elegant and gracious in her speech – a girl of style.

The demands of disease and pressure of money brought her among us. She was blessed with a friend whom she cared for lovingly but she used to worry about the companionship. Her sense of humour helped us to smooth over that pain. She had dreams of helping the youth and organising parish projects and housekeeping for the priest.

On Good Friday she gave me a twenty pound note. 'You gave me this last year for some milk and cigarettes' she said. I refused, saying that the money was a present, but she insisted, 'I promised.' She was found dead in Easter week. Her note said 'she loved those she was leaving.' I believe Eileen's Good Friday is now a glorious Easter. I ask her to help us – she knows and understands.

'A Servant is not greater than his master' *Jn 15:18-21*

Holy Saturday

I am a spark of fire from the mystery of God, shrouded in darkness but a light of life. My present base is this world, but I am called to journey with others, to build God's kingdom on earth and reach it's fulfilment in heaven.

In the Vigil readings, we have looked back through the family album of the people in search of God. In the Vigil baptism, we have welcomed a new member into our searching community. At the Vigil Mass, we have celebrated together our journey of faith, and we go on now to love God and serve one another in the ups and downs of everyday life, strengthened by the Bread of Christ.

Easter Monday

You can catch joy at Easter time, in the colours of children, the dress of nature, new flowers, new birds, new lambs.

There is another way of making joy that Jesus teaches: that is to have an eye to compliment others. It can be a word, a hug, a gift, a handshake. It is best to begin with those nearest to us.

Jesus takes the initiative in complimenting. He makes the first move. 'There, coming to meet them, was Jesus. 'Greetings!' he said.'

There, coming to meet them, was Jesus. 'Greetings!' he said.

Mt 28:8-15

Easter Tuesday

In the divorce court a sobbing wife said to her partner, 'When you were a prisoner of war in Poland we were really happy and in love. Now when we are together we hate one another, and life is a bitterness.'

We all need space to be ourselves, and we cannot be absorbed or smothered without damage. Mary Magdalen was the first to experience Easter love. She was taught by Jesus not to cling.

Real love cannot be over-possessive. It has to respect the freedom and identity of the other person. I cannot always have my way.

Jesus said to Mary, 'Do not cling to me.' *Jn 20:11-18*

Easter Wednesday

We watch TV; people are present to us but not in the same place with us. We look at the photographs, make a phone-call, imagine and dream. There is a presence, even if the person is far away and cannot be seen.

After the resurrection, the Lord chose new ways to be present to us. He reveals his presence to us in the compassion, caring and love of his followers. When Peter healed the crippled beggar, Christ was there

When friendship, welcome, hospitality happen, Christ is there.

He walked by their side but something prevented them from recognising him. *Lk 24:13-25*

Easter Thursday

Sr Brid McKenna is well known for her healing mission. She insists that Christ is the one who heals. 'The Mass is healing,' she says. 'The word of God in Scripture is healing.'

The friends of Jesus try to explain this healing presence of Christ. They say that he is present in the 'Breaking of Bread.' That includes work, which is often called 'making bread.' Work at home means preparing bread and sharing bread. Feeding the hungry means giving bread.

When we 'break the bread' together at Mass, Jesus is present to renew, encourage and forgive us in our celebration in his name.

Jesus at the Breaking of Bread. *Lk 24:35-48*

Easter Friday

Leo is a month dead today. My thoughts go to his brave wife Carmel. She is passing through an ordeal of pain, a sense of loss. This is not of her making.

The Easter story today tells too of a 'passing through ordeal. The bottom has fallen out of Peter's world.

He says – 'I'll go back fishing.' His friends say 'we'll come with you.' All night they find nothing, nothing... Yet the Lord is present on the shore at dawn. 'Try the net again for fish' Jesus says. It happens. Fish are found. 'Bring some to share in the meal. Come, have breakfast.' Their minds and hearts inquire 'Who are you' He steps foward offering bread.

It is better to ask 'when' is God, rather than 'where.' God is, when anyone cares, has a word, offers a hand, tries again. God is, when friends rally around, and make allowances. God is, when we search and cry out 'who are you God.' God is when, he steps foward to offer us bread of consolation. May the Mass help us to pass through our ordeals in the strength of him who passed through before us and beckons us to shore.

'Jesus then stepped foward, took the Bread and gave to them.'

Jn 21: 1-14

Easter Saturday

The old psychologist was half daft with learning. He was very dependent on the bottle. He was estranged in marriage but he had an extraordinary kindness that redeemed him and made him lovable. He ranted and cursed about his weakness, but a lady patient liked his kindness and sought his company.

There is a resurrected presence of Christ in kindness. Kindness is often parcelled in human weakness. Mary Magdalen, Christ's first love of Easter, was kindness parcelled in human weakness.

Jesus appeared first to Mary Magdalen from whom he cast out seven devils. *Mk 16:9-15*

Second Week of Easter: Monday

Rosemary Conley's book, *Hip and Thigh Diet*, is a best-seller. She developed a serious gall-bladder problem. The low-fat diet needed to cope with this also coped with extra pounds on hips and thighs.

She says, 'I am a committed Christian. I feel very strongly that the Lord controls my life. I came to see religion as a power for living. Before, life was all about money and success. Now I think differently. My success is not really my doing. I feel like an ambassador from God, helping people to live healthier and happier lives. The life-giving power of God's spirit blows constantly.'

The wind blows where it pleases. *Jn 3:1-8*

Second Week of Easter: Tuesday

'Transitions make up life.' So a woman writer wrote, speaking of Easter. She said we cannot stay in empty tombs or keep thinking about empty tombs. We must learn from Mary Magdalen. We say that life goes on, but we sometimes don't like the tensions, challenges and growing pains that carry new life. Holding grudges, keeping up bitterness, is an empty tomb. Preoccupation with jealousy or envy is an empty tomb. Fear of failure, fear to accept one's weaknesses and fear of 'accelerating birthdays,' are empty tombs. Too much bottle or pill can be empty tombs. Mary Magdalen left the empty tomb for love of Jesus, and was strengthened by him.

Born in the Spirit. *Jn 3:7-18*

Second Week of Easter: Wednesday

Some people get depressed about birthdays because they're getting old. We can confuse getting old with liveliness and youthfulness. The Easter poet says youthfulness is in the mind and heart. We are always young inside.

The poet in his mid-fifties says he delights to hear the birds singing at 5 am. Despite all the ups and downs of life, they are ever faithful, with sounds of hope. He sees and hears more with maturing years. Openness of mind and heart is the secret of youthfulness. Insight makes for liveliness.

I asked a teenager which Disco she liked best. She said, 'It is not the place, it is what you make of it yourself that is best.'

Tell the people about this new life. *Acts 5:17-26*

Second Week of Easter: Thursday

A young writer who rediscovered God said that in religion there was too much stress on learning and not enough emphasis on witnessing. I think he meant that there can be too much talking, and not enough Christian action or desire to share our treasured message. 'We are all baptised Christians,' he said, 'not just the religious.'

In our common baptism,
may God the Father's gift of caring come alive in us;
may God the Son's gift of sharing come alive in us;
may God the Spirit's gift of faithfulness come alive in us.

We are witnesses — we and the Holy Spirit. *Acts 5:7-32*

Second Week of Easter: Friday

An African sister had to speak on Mission Sunday. She said that there was once a famine among her people. Africans always share food when a visitor calls. This farmer had his last bits and pieces of food for his family boiling in a pot. He saw a neighbour coming to the house. He whipped the pot from the fire, sat down on it, and covered it with his cloak to hide the food. The visitor stayed a long time. The farmer burnt his backside on the hot pot, and the food was a mess and no good to eat. She said, 'If we don't share our food with others it won't do us any good either.'

Not enough for all. Then Jesus took the bread. *Jn 6:1-15*

Second Week of Easter: Saturday

Barbara fell and broke her arm. She was recovering nicely when she fell and broke her other arm. She met the priest in hospital and said, 'Why does God do this to me?' The priest said, 'God wants to test you Barbara.' She wasn't too happy with that answer and said naughty things about religion.

God does not send us troubles nor does he promise to take them away. But he does promise to help us through . When bad things happen to good people, God is present. God does walk with us but we don't recognise him.

Barbara's family and neighbours were very supportive. She praised the hospital staff. She even joked that she wished this had happened years ago because now her husband was calling her 'dearie', preparing and serving meals, taking her on tours. When one door closes, God opens other doors.

A strong wind was blowing. They saw Jesus walking on the water coming near the boat. Don't be afraid. *Jn 6:16-22*

Third Week of Easter: Monday

There was a man who believed that God would intervene directly to save him, in any crisis. He got seriously ill. The wife said, 'We'll get the doctor.' He said, 'No! God will save me.' 'We'll get some penicillin tablets.' He said, 'No! God will save me.' 'We'll call the hospital.' He said, 'No! God will save me.' He died, met God and said to God, 'You let me down. I was always religious.' God said, 'I came to you three times and you said "No!" I sent the doctor. I sent the penicillin. I sent the hospital.'

Jesus had a problem with miracles. They were signs of God's help and presence now and hints of heaven. They are around us all the time and they are not magic. The penicillin that cures, the nurse who cares, the next door neighbour, the wine in the bottle, the food on the table. Jesus' miracle stories very often end up with the word 'home'. Being at home, the everyday miracle.

You are looking for me because you have all you wanted, not because you understood my miracles. *Jn 6:16*

Third Week of Easter: Tuesday

Fr Rolheiser tells the story of a youngster who had a row with his father, left home and Church, and went sexually free. Twenty years later he was rejected by a lover. Deeply hurt and depressed he decided to make up with his father. He returned home and was reconciled. His father died a month later. He felt the need to be active in Church but met a priest who didn't really understand his need for re-assurance. He decided to go to Mass and receive Holy Communion. He explains the deep peace he experienced and the sense of forgiveness when he received Communion.

The Mass is the great sign of God's reconciliation and forgiveness. Our Father always calls, 'Take and eat.'

He who comes to me will never be hungry. *Jn 6:35*

Third Week of Easter: Wednesday

Irene, a Russian girl, was imprisoned for writing poetry. Although not a believer, she found God in her suffering, hunger and torture. She even prayed for her tormentors. 'When I get to heaven,' she said, 'I will write my best poetry, because I will be more creative, when I can see more clearly.' She said, 'I will be curious to see how God recreates, refashions, refines people who do such evil to others. There is no hell made by God. People make their own hell but somehow God goes into hell and redeems. These words of Jesus I like to take to heart: 'I will never turn away anyone. It is his will ... that I should not lose any of those he has given, but should raise them all to life.'

I will never turn away anyone who comes to me nor lose all he has given me, but raise them all to life. *Jn 6:37*

Third Week of Easter: Thursday

'No one comes to me unless the Father draws them,' my friend said. Life goes in cycles; we can't anticipate. We have to wait for wisdom. Getting the Leaving Cert was a highlight, an ambition then. Life would be great at University or with a job and my own money, but there were snags – other exams. The girl friends brought joy but decisions too. 'When I get qualified and get a better job, life will be good,' but there were new hurdles and obstacles. Marriage snags and money scarce. What is the right decision?

There doesn't seem enough time. Wedding day comes, mortgage grows, children arrive. The pace hots up. There are new demands. Now, twenty years on, I find I'm living the same experiences for my children. Life is indeed a coming and going, a journey, and God can be refound or experienced as more real in a later cycle of life. An old prayer means more now; appreciation of values encouraged by the Church take on new meaning: 'The travelling Ethiopian was rediscovering God through Philip.'

Third Week of Easter: Friday

A woman begged at the street corner in Paris. The poet Rilke passed everyday. He threw her a coin. She never raised her head. Then one day he stopped. He put a rose in her hand. She raised her head and smiled. She never went back to beg again. That moment of dignity, that moment of saying you are of value, you are worthwhile, gave a new image of self to her and changed her attitude.

That is how I like to see Communion. The Bread of Life not so much given to be adorned, but there to give us worth, a dignity, a value, despite all our weaknesses and limitations. In the strength of that food we can smile at ourselves and smile at the world. It is bread given for our sake because of God's goodness.

'This is the bread come down from heaven... anyone who eats will live – *Jn 6:52-59*

Third Week of Easter: Saturday

The first arrivals for the Christening were two elderly blind people. Their white guiding-sticks were like two white candles, keeping watch during the celebration. They were obviously so happy to celebrate this day. John lost his sight when a child. Mary his wife lost her sight when she was seven. They laughed about the happiness of their marriage of thirty years. 'What is your special secret?' I asked. John said, 'Trust in God.' Mary said, 'Acceptance.'

Peter's stories of people helped, healed and consoled, are born from trust in Jesus who never leaves his people, and acceptance of human weakness in all its shades. From these two sources, new blessings spring forth to heal our world.

Lord, to whom shall we go? *Jn 6:60-69*

Fourth Week of Easter: Monday

Two people were looking at a garden. One said, 'Aren't the weeds terrible?' The other said, 'Aren't the flowers beautiful?' The way we see, the attitude of mind, is pretty mysterious. This fascinates me about Jesus – the way he could see life.

A little child in the crowd, powerless and of no consequence, is important to him. He takes the child in arms. In a beggar on the roadside, he sees beauty. In a woman in distress, he sees a heart of gold.

Age has its blessings in that we can think back and see our small mindedness, our pompous know-all-ish and judgemental attitudes. The Church tries to renew her vision of God, people and the world all the time. Peter is having his vision and view of life renewed and enlarged today.

All that exists is good. What we make of it is another story.

What God has made clean you have no right to call profane.

Acts 11:1-18

Fourth Week of Easter: Tuesday

We've often felt hurt when the thanks that we deserved was not spoken. I was advised once never to expect thanks. If it happens, it's a perk! That person was saying to me, 'Whatever you do in life, do it because it is worth doing in God's name. it may be a job of work , helping the parish and community or going to Mass.' A lot of doing in life is underground and un-noticed.

The notion of a Jesus doing miracles most of his life is false. Most of his life was underground. We have no records of almost thirty years. His passion and death, on the surface, produced nothing but failure. Jesus during the trial seems so passive, inactive, nothing to say or do. Yet, because of this, he is acclaimed by the soldier. 'This is surely the Son of God.'

Somehow, his great works are in ordinary weakness, inactivity, painful waiting, journeying on.

The works I do in my Father's name are my witness. *Jn 10:22-30*

Fourth Week of Easter: Wednesday

We had a little get-together in Church last evening. The little ones called it, 'Celebrating their First Forgiveness.' The parent presented the child to the priest to celebrate First Forgiveness. A child told a story of Jesus, other children said 'Thank You' and 'Sorry' prayers.

We are introduced to God, generally, by a parent, in a person-to-person way - not by a crowd. Paul and Barnabas brought Andrew. Jesus is a one-to-one person. He touches the individual.

The little ones teach us that 'Thank You' comes first. 'I am alive; I am here; God loves me.' 'Sorry' and sin is in second place and not meant to be an obsession or pre-occupation. 'I have come to save. Let the people praise.'

I have come not to condemn the world but to save it.   *Jn 12:44-50*

Fourth Week of Easter: Thursday

I marvel at a friend of mine. He always loves to sing a song. His prayer with the sick is often a song sung. A song opens the heart, reveals the person.

The Australian singer, Pete Carney writes, 'Lord you can make me (into) a song.' He imagines that there is the making of a song in each of us. We have power to enliven, brighten our world and the people we meet. We are God's ambassadors, or songsters, with gifts to help, heal, listen, care and share, as we travel along the road of life.

David was a songster. God calls him a man after my own heart. 'I will sing for ever of your love O Lord. The hand of God is with me, his arm makes me strong. I say you are my Father, my God - the Lord that saves me.'

I will sing forever of your love, O Lord. *Ps 88*

Fourth Week of Easter: Friday

A man said jokingly and gratefully that he thought that he was going to die last year in hospital. 'I had my bags packed,' he said, 'but the train didn't come.'

I have heard life and death compared to a train journey. We don't have to worry about the train coming. God Our Father will come in his own time. Some people travel short train journeys, others travel a longer distance. But for each, the journey is complete – mission accomplished.

In God's plan, distance of years doesn't seem to have the same value that we think. Jesus knows our worries about the life and death train. He encourages us. 'Let not your hearts be troubled. I shall return ... be with you.' He will do the driving.

I shall return and take you. Do not let your hearts be troubled.

Jn 14:1-16

Fourth Week after Easter: Saturday

When I was a youngster, there was one boy in our street who owned a football. He wouldn't let others play with his football. Sometimes, in the middle of a match, if his side was losing, he'd pick up the ball and run home.

A football is made for fun, not just for one person. It is made to be shared. The psychologists say that if we hold on to things or persons too much it is bad for us. We are insecure, seriously afraid to lose our football.

Jesus understands the human condition and is always wanting to help us. He says we have a Father in heaven who cares. There is more than one football. We can afford to use God's blessings without fear of losing out. The greatest blessings are yet to come, so we can be carefree and enjoy life, which is God's gift.

It is the Father living in me that is doing the work. *Jn 14:7-14*

Fifth Week of Easter: Monday

We hear about 'doing the Leaving.' We are a people always leaving. That is why we call life a journey – going from one stage to another stage of living. The Christian traveller can see a lot of meaning in this leaving business, especially leavings that are forced on us – like weakening health, growing years, changing job or house. Parents constantly leave their own wishes aside for the sake of others in the family. So the good Lord stresses this word 'leaving' a lot: 'Leave your father and mother ... cling to your wife.' Too much intereference by family in marriages is a failure to leave people to be themselves.

Jesus always seems to be leaving, even at the height of success. He says, 'Let us go elsewhere.' He is present in the 'elsewheres' of life. Leaving 'all' they followed him. An old retired teacher leaving his school and home said, 'I'm sad, but there will always be a friend if one makes the effort to seek one, to go out and to find.'

Mass celebrates the leavings of life, and promises strength and encouragement as we pass daily from experience to experience. Christ is our passover, rewarding a hundredfold in this life and in eternal life.

I have said these things to you when still with you.   *Jn 14:21-26*

Fifth Week of Easter: Tuesday

Her boy of twelve was killed in an accident. 'It was unthinkable that I would ever lose him,' she said. 'But now, years on, I'm at peace. I go to the graveside sometimes. I talk to him about his brothers and sisters, about what's happening and what he would be like now, twelve years later. I feel close, even though I cannot demonstrate love in a physical way. But you don't always have to hug and kiss to show love or be physically present. I have no regrets. Love is stronger than ever. I was not consoled by people who told me to thank God for a saint in heaven. I was greatly consoled by Cardinal Ó Fiaich who put his arms around me and said, 'I have no words. I'd be shattered too.' But God must have some plan that we can't understand.'

I give peace the world cannot give. If you loved me you'd be glad to know that I am going to the Father.

Jn 14:27–31

Fifth Week of Easter: Wednesday

Dostoyevsky and Solzhenitzyn were two great Russian writers. Both struggled with religious belief. Both said that in life, if we humans don't worship or praise some supreme being outside ourselves, we end up worshipping ourselves, or the State Government. That is idolatry and a dehumanising of people, and that is disastrous.

Jesus puts us humans in proper context. We are in relationship to God, like branches of the tree. We cannot really separate from God. We are dependent. But the relationship is not remote. Ours is a loving relationship with Our Father. There is a pruning and pain in life that we don't like or understand, but it is part of God's life in abundance because we are all in God's hands.

You are the branches. *Jn 15:1-8*

Fifth Week of Easter: Thursday

If there are too many rules at home, there is unhappiness and tensions. Pre-occupation with rules can take the good out of life. Jesus says rules are meant to be life-giving. Life is good. There is a joy element in life. When we think of God, do we think first, 'rule giver' or 'life giver'?

The Church always struggles with this tension. Paul fights against extra rules that make life more difficult for people. I found the Confirmation class quite rule-conscious. They said missing Mass on Sunday is a sin, breaks the law. I'd like them to say, 'It is an opportunity missed to share together, to support people, at home and far away, to be friendly, to be more human.'

Is forgiveness a humiliation to be observed, or an opportunity to be more human, realising one's own limitations but also being thankful for talents that can give joy to the world?

That my joy may be in you and your joy complete. *Jn 15:9-11*

Fifth Week of Easter: Friday

A man and a woman were celebrating fifty years of marriage. The man said, 'Not only was Mary my special partner through life, she was also my best friend.' They say that if we have a few friends in life we are blessed. What a fantastic compliment Jesus gave us: 'You are my friends.'

What is the secret of a friend? I think it's being able to confide, to say the way I am to another and not feel rejected. We're afraid to let people know the kind of shocking thoughts we can have. A friend is someone who understands and reacts with sympathetic sighs and a kindly 'Sure. I understand, of course.' A friend is more a listener than a counsellor.

I call you friends because I have made known to you everything.
Jn 15:12-17

Fifth Week of Easter: Saturday

A packed house, all age groups, prolonged applause, made me think about Lee Dunne's 'Goodbye to the Hill.' Perhaps the play touches human emotions in us, that we're ashamed to express openly, so there is a kind of forgiveness in the language, circumstances and humour. A young man wants to make it good in life. He has an ideal, but he is dragged down and destroyed by the cynicism of George. Gargle is George's priority. Life is a game, a mess. Loyalty a joke. Outwit the system. The young man is torn apart having to lie about his work, having to lie about his relationships because his mother would not understand. She wanted the perfect boy. He has to lie about himself.

He looses the girl he really wanted to love. There must be more to life than this, so to find himself to be a man, to be more human, it must be Goodbye to the Hill. Leaving is not always a sign of failure, it has also the seed of rebirth, resurrection, new found values and freedom.

Because you do not belong to the world... it hates you. *Jn 15:18–21*

Sixth Week of Easter: Monday

I like the story of about the seagull's first flight. Safe in the cliff nest, high over the sea, he refused to fly. His brothers and sisters had made the jump and were enjoying life. He'd take a little run to the edge of the nest, look down on the sea miles below, flap his wings and retire in fear. The mother teased the seagull out of the nest with hunger. She kept dangling pieces of fish in front of him until one day he jumped. With a loud scream he fell downwards into space. His mother swooped near him. He heard the swish of her wings. He was in terror, but only for a moment. Suddenly his wings spread out. The wind rushed against his breast feathers, under his stomach, against his wings. He wasn't falling now but soaring with delight. The Spirit broods over all of life and helps us through risks, fear, pains and expulsions.

They will expel you. *Jn 15:26-64*

Sixth Week of Easter: Tuesday

I spot little tears of joy and sadness at First Communion time. This tiny mite of seven years ago (a bundle of promise then) now unravelling fast into a new world of new experiences. There's no stopping them. 'Endless energy,' we say. 'They're growing away from us,' they say, 'from the time of learning to walk – like the little bird finding its wings. It moves away in excitement to capture the world. The nest renews the strength to keep flying away.'

This growing away happens all the time. This growing up, leaving stage after stage of life, experience after experience, is called a special journey, a pilgrimage, and is blessed by Christ. He journeyed through all human experiences – birth, life, love, death and beyond. He assures us that our everyday goings and comings, leavings and takings, are in the hands of God's Spirit.

It is for your good that I am going. *Jn 16:15-11*

Sixth Week of Easter: Wednesday

I'm glad I went to Athens once to see the Areopagus. The greatest speech of all time was made by Paul there, to a kind of university audience, intelligent, proud of achievement, religious-minded. Paul said, 'You worship God without knowing it, for in God we live, move, exist. God is not man-made.'

I often say to myself and others that the first worship, first Mass, is living and caring at home. Already this morning you have got children fed, ready for school. Maybe baby didn't sleep well. It was a long night. We've tried to cope with the moods and manners of others. Taking on the day's work and challenges, keeping house, planning, shopping, celebrating, keeping an eye to family needs, parish needs, community needs, personal needs.

Jesus blessed every human experience. He is present in all the bits and pieces of our living. His resurrected Spirit is among us, kind of unknown to us.

You already worship God without knowing it ...
it is in him we live, move and exist. *Acts 17:15-22*

Sixth Week of Easter: Ascension Thursday

Irene was imprisoned in Russia for writing poetry. Amidst cruelty and hunger she found God. She was interviewed on TV about heaven. She said, 'When I get to heaven I will write my best poetry, because I will see and understand more clearly. I'll be more creative. I will be curious to see how God recreates, renews, transforms my torturers.'

Nobody knows what heaven is like. Ascension Day is a hint. It is not a dead end, a full stop, collecting the prize. It is a mission accomplished, not a mission ended. Ascension is more like the day baby is born. Achievement - yes, a great human achievement – but a beginning too. In a sense, life is really beginning now - plenty of activity, on-going growth and life.

Christ is now more active, more alive, flooding the world with his Spirit, interceding always, not leaving us orphans, working fulltime. Life is not about resting on our laurels, burying our talent, but about passing on life in all kinds of ways of caring, helping, encouraging, forgiving.

When he ascended he gave gifts to mankind. *Eph 4:1-13*

Sixth Week of Easter: Friday

We all have pictures, paintings and photos at home. When we look at a picture, it tells us something about the artist. Paul Henry likes clouds, mountains, sky colour. God's best art-piece is the human person.

In the great human achievement of child-birth, there is pain and joy. That's a mix we live with. That is a mix Jesus lived with. That is a mix we are helped with, by the Spirit that Jesus sends. There is pain and beauty in growing and the Spirit strengthens our spirit.

She forgets the suffering in her joy
that a child has been born into the world. *Jn 16:20-23*

Sixth Week of Easter: Saturday

The teacher was explaining to the little ones that prayer is not just talking. It is listening to one's own heart, the heart of others, the heart of nature, the wisdom and creativeness of people over centuries in our world.

The prisoner, Anatoli Levitin, said his greatest gift and privilege was being able to pray, to tap in on God. He found life bursting in him, 'Me, an unimportant, tired old man. I prayed - in imagination attending services with congregations over the world. I prayed in my own words for all kinds of people. The whole universe became my home.'

Maybe when Jesus says, 'Ask in my name, you will receive his joy,' he is telling us that the very asking is a blessing that fills a human need. Asking is like breathing. The very breathing is blessing also. It sustains life. The asking is God's way of blessing us. His arm does not have to be twisted. Jesus' pattern of prayer so often begins with thanks, and there is often more concern for others than for self. Not so much, 'Do it my way,' as, 'God help me through doing it your way.' 'With the help of God,' we say.

Ask and you will receive
So your joy will be complete. *Jn 16:23-28*

Seventh Week of Easter: Monday

I saw a film about a team that climbed Mt Everest. The heroes were praised for conquering the mountain heights through desperate hours of danger in snow and ice, against the odds. The leader said, 'We didn't conquer the mountain, we conquered ourselves.'

I think that he meant that battling with oneself means trying to live with others, coping with the unexpected, trying to enter another person's joy.

Conquering self was misunderstood in some religions. Discipline is an important virtue, but it is not number one. Love is the important gift. Love is Christ's way. We learn discipline from loving. Trying to love involves struggle. Jesus did not look for pain or sacrifice, but, because he loved and respected people, pain and suffering came his way. He said, 'Have courage. I have conquered the world.' He is the Lamb of God who takes away the sin of the world.

Be brave. I have conquered the world. *Jn 16:29-33*

Seventh Week of Easter: Tuesday

After visiting Africa, my friend explained that an African doesn't exchange a name lightly. The name is told when one wants to be a friend. There is trust and companionship in revealing the name.

Jesus says, 'I've made known the name of my Father to you.' It is saying that God wants to love us, wants our friendship, seeks intimacy with us. 'You are my friends.'

The Spirit makes God intimate in our lives, and lets us 'see' his heart, his mind, his openness to us, his wonder, his mystery, his constant forgiveness in every ray of light and every breath of life we breathe. It is on-going education. There is always more to see.

The Spirit recreates us too through the mystery of dying. Paul says, 'I've no idea what will happen to me.' But he is pleased to be an ambassador of God's love and purpose.

I have made your name known. *Jn 17:1-11*

Seventh Week of Easter: Wednesday

I met a woman at a funeral. She said, 'I don't understand Mass, but I go. I light six candles every Sunday for the four children, myself and Brendan. I say, 'Now God, it is over to you. You know all the needs, anxieties, difficulties. Help them through.'

I think that was the way Jesus prayed for us. 'Keep them. Help them to make a better world. Protect them from evil.'

It is still the way Christ prays in us all the time, whether we know it or not.

Yesterday I met a mother with a little baby in a buggy. Babies have extraordinary looks. The baby tried to gurgle out sounds to me. The mother said, 'She talks to everybody.' The Spirit is always talking in everybody.

Keep those you have given me.
Do not to remove them from the world.
Protect them from evil. *Jn 17:11-19*

Seventh Week of Easter: Thursday

The Spirit of God was present at the making of the world, 'hovering over the waters of the deep, sunbeams, stars and mountains.' The Spirit has always been present, renewing, recreating, refashioning people and places.

Whit or Pentecost is not a first appearance of the Spirit of God. It is more a celebration of his presence in all life - like a birthday.

All humans are like tourists in God's world. Maybe the Christian is a tourist with a map, but we know many tourists who can do as well, and better, without a map. The Christian map tells us God's purpose. We come from the Father in love, through Christ in whose image we are inspired by the Spirit. All that exists is stamped in that pattern, is on that journey.

The Bible is God's picture-book, showing the family of Father, Son, Spirit and showing me my place in their company. It is a family full of diversity.

Father, I want those you have given me to be with me where I am.

Jn 17:20-26

Seventh Week of Easter: Friday

People often say, 'I don't understand Mass, but I go.' Others say, 'I don't have to go to Mass to be a good Christian.'

There is truth in all this. There is a wondrous mystery about Mass, because it is a presence of Christ in the gathering of people. How, we don't know. Mass can be celebrated in a thousand different ways: the prisoner in the cell, king in the palace, pope in the basilica, mothers and babies in distracted moods.

Jesus tells Peter about two basic ingredients in every Mass gathering, no matter how vast the congregation, how long the Mass, how exciting the priest, or how mixed the attendance. 'After the meal Jesus said to Peter, 'Do you love me? ... feed my lambs, feed my sheep.' Love of God, or God's love for us, is expressed in concern for human persons and human needs. This is the basic Mass ingredient.

'Through this sacred meal, you give us strength to please you and to care for one another. Help all who follow Jesus to work for peace and bring happiness to others.'

Do you love me? Feed my lambs. *Jn 21:15-19*

Seventh Week after Easter: Saturday

If we get a bad apple we don't give up eating fruit. If we are disappointed with the hairstylist, or breadman, we don't give up living. Yet sometimes it is said that, because of a clash or falling out with the priest or sister, 'I'm giving up God.'

What has poor God got to do with it? God is the most maligned of persons. Maybe we use subtle excuses to opt out of responsibility. 'I don't give. I don't support, because I don't like what so and so said or so and so did.' It is like the lady who refused to contribute to the swimming pool because she might never use it. She forgets that the youngsters using it are well occupied rather than harassing others. We might never use the Fire Brigade, but it is good to support its usefulness.

We have a personal relationship with God. What another does is his business, but I have my business and duty. Jesus says, 'What does it matter to you what he does? You follow me.'

What does it matter to you? You are to follow me. *Jn 21:20-25*

Pentecost Vigil

The baby gurgles and smiles. The mother says, 'She talks to everybody.' St Paul says, 'The Spirit speaks in our spirit.' The spirit is always talking.

A little boy asked me, 'Would you like a kick of my football?' All good thoughts come from the Holy Spirit.

First Holy Communion Day is full of joy, colour, beauty, achievement. Even rows and break-ups are made up for that day. The Spirit of God is alive.

Rose, the widow, told me that she left her husband once. There was a falling out. She remembers that there was a mouse in the house at the time. Her husband prompted the children to phone her. She could hear him whispering to the children, 'Ask Mam to come back.' She was delighted and looked forward to hugs and kisses of welcome when she returned. When she arrived, full of anticipation, he said, 'Rose, I caught the mouse.' Reconciling language of the Spirit, in strange words.

Come Holy Spirit, fill the hearts of the faithful.

Note to the Reader:

On the Monday after Pentecost Sunday, we return to Ordinary Time until the end of the year. There are thirty-four weeks in ordinary time and the thirty-fourth week is always the week ending on the Saturday before the First Sunday of Advent. To decide which week to start with after Pentecost, we must work backwards from the week before the First Sunday of Advent. This works out as follows for the next few years:

1993 Week 9 page 71

1994 Week 8 page 68

1995 Week 9 page 71

1996 Week 8 page 68

1997 Week 7 page 65

1998 Week 9 page 71

1999 Week 8 page 68

2000 Week 10 page 73

Ordinary Time Week 1: Monday

The stamp of Christ is on everything that exists, on rocks which are 350 million years old, on stars which are billions of light years in space, on the perfection and colour of the wings of a bird.

It is said that St Patrick made a circle about himself everyday because he believed that he was encircled and surrounded by God's love in every face he saw, in all of nature, in all the events of living.

There is one world – God's world – stamped in the image of Jesus Christ.

The Father has appointed the Son to inherit everything and, through him, he made everything there is. *Heb 1:1-6*

Ordinary Time Week 1: Tuesday

Father Hughes, in his book *God of Surprises* talks about the conflicting desires that are part and parcel of every human heart. We must look at this inner world of conflict in order to see our good world. There are convulsions of anger, resentment, bitterness, jealousy, disappointment, and moods that change daily, even hourly. That is us.

The very gifts that are our blessings often carry a dark streak of weakness. He was a great preacher, a great organiser, but you couldn't talk to him! A great charity person, but forgot his own! Great at going to Mass, but a hard critic! Great with strangers, but a devil at home!

We need a healing presence when we are faced with 'the unclean spirit that throws us into convulsions.' (Mic 1:21-28) Jesus calls our burdens his burdens too. He promises to help us.

Even the unclean spirits obey him. *Mk 1:21-28*

Ordinary Time Week 1: Wednesday

A young girl volunteered to be a hospital friend. She was assigned a little boy whose father was unknown and whose mother had Aids. She explains her fears in the early days just holding the little boy in her arms, but as time went on both became relaxed and content. The little boy was never left alone without company and in the later days of his life this little girl and her friend arranged never to leave him on his own. He died at fourteen moths.

The girl was deeply saddened and wondered where was God in all this, allowing 'an innocent' to endure this suffering. There was no complete answer. Yet, the heart of God is present in the caring attention people showed this little child. He is present in the lovliness of a young girl who volunteered for this work and found great peace in sharing the burden of another. The psychiatrist said that the pain and trauma of life, of separation, break-up in marriage relationships is like 'possession'– say sorry for your trouble, shake a hand, give a hug.

They brought to Him… those who were possessed. *Mk 1:29–39*

Ordinary Time Week 1: Thursday

I have found that children at Mass love shaking hands. I have also found that their handshakes give something special that heals and encourages. They like being touched.

I like holding a person's hand when celebrating the sacrament of God's forgiveness. Jesus used his hands a lot to touch, to comfort, to help, to welcome.

When Jesus touched and cured the leper, the leper was able to go back to his family and friends again as an equal.

All sacraments are meant to put us in touch with one another, in touch with the blessings of life, and in touch with God our Father. *Mk 1:40-45*

Ordinary Time Week 1: Friday

The children in school told me that Jesus blessed the sick man on the stretcher because his friends wouldn't give up.

It is consoling to know that our efforts for others do really reach the heart of God. Nothing is forgotten. This is expressed in the way we celebrate the Sacrament of the Sick. It is not for the priest on his own but includes all the caring people of the community, family carers, medical and nursing carers, neighbours, visitors, administration, telephone service, shop service, floor service.

Seeing their (his friends) faith. *Mk 2:1-12*

Ordinary Time Week 1: Saturday

Fr Hughes tells about good Old Uncle George who lived in a big mansion. He was very powerful and intelligent. The children were brought to visit Uncle George. He had a beard and never smiled. He brought the children down into the basement of the mansion. There were big steel doors which he unlocked. They could hear people screaming. Then they saw fires and people in the fires. Uncle George said, 'If you don't come here every week to visit me and if you don't love me with your whole heart and mind and strength that is where you go too.'

On the way home the children clutched the hands of parents in fear. The parents said, 'Isn't Uncle George good - don't you like him?' They hated the monster, but were afraid to say it to their parents, lest they go to that terrible place too.

Jesus came to destroy that image of God, but what a battle he had.

'Jesus not only sits with sinners but even eats with them, but we won't have that kind of God.' *Mk 2:13-17*

Ordinary Time Week 2: Monday

Joy in life and religion began for me in the days when I tried believing that God really loved me, warts and all. It began to dawn on me that God loved me first - all was gift as the Holy Book says. I didn't have to force his love or do things to pacify him, to gain his favour.

In my seminary days, the stress seemed to be on getting the right answers in exams, on knowing the rules, and on suppressing yourself, even your natural gifts. It was 'the times' as we say and no blame to those who were doing their best.

Thank God I've tasted 'bridegroom religion' and new wine in my lifetime, despite all the problems.

As long as they have the bridegroom with them they could not think of fasting. *Mk 2 18-22*

Ordinary Time Week 2: Tuesday

There is a story in my birthday, in my anniversary, in winning that medal. We like to retell our stories and we do it all with celebration and we blow out the candles on the birthday cake. We lift the glasses. We drink out of the winner's cup. It all makes us more human, more friendly, more together. There is a past, present and future.

The sabbath and the Sunday is also about 'my story'. Loved into life and family by God Our Father, we keep telling the story. Loved through life with a million blessings, we celebrate those and we support and care for each other in the power of God. The sabbath is our story to be celebrated. It was made for us.

The sabbath was made for man. *Mk 2:23-28*

Ordinary Time Week 2: Wednesday

The children loved the story of the man with a withered hand. One boy said that the man was mean and greedy and kept his hand in his pocket when it came his turn to buy a drink - and it got withered. So Jesus shouted at him, 'Stand up stretch out your hand.'

Whenever friendship was exchanged, a friend used to say, 'May the giving hand never wither.'

Brian Keenan, who was imprisoned for years as a hostage, spoke powerfully about his chained hands. These hands, he said, are gifted to save, to comfort, to beautify the world. They can also fight and destroy life.

Stand up! Stretch out your hand! *Mk 3:1-6*

Ordinary Time Week 2: Thursday

The demands of young children, family life, pressure of work, can be crushing. We are not good at being kind to ourselves. The emotional demands of a child can become almost obsessive. A mature mother said regretfully to me recently that to spend twenty years of life, 24 hours a day, absorbed in house and home is madness.

I am me, a special son or daughter of God our Father. I must stop playing God and make breaks, little treats, little silences for myself, so that I can be a more human person, in touch with myself and with others in kindness and caring. When we're crushed we're not able to touch anyone.

To keep him from being crushed. *Mk 3:7-12*

Ordinary Time Week 2: Friday

Companion is a very soothing word. It is made up of two words cum, which means with and panis which means bread. A companion is someone you sit with over a meal and share thoughts and experiences. That's how Jesus describes his relationship with us. We are his companions.

That is the good news of religion: that God is our friend and we are his friends and companions. Many people could not accept this idea of God, but the weak and sinners could – because they realised all was gift, we're always dependent.

They were to be his companions. *Mk 3:13-19*

Ordinary Time Week 2: Saturday

When I was ten years old, my father got involved in politics. A young man cycled into our village and said he wanted to work for people, especially the less well off. My father gave him a chair to make his speech at the crossroads, and he campaigned for him as well. That man was elected to government and topped the poll year after year until his death. He was a people's man.

The sad memory is that his arrival in our village hastened my mother's death. She was shy and sensitive and felt very embarrassed by my father's involvement with this young unpredictable enthusiast. Her family were very conservative people and would have hinted at their disapproval. 'He'd be better off looking after his own. We wouldn't mind if he could afford it ...'

It all reminds me of Jesus, the young enthusiast, coming to his home town with all his followers. Mary's relations think he is mad, but Mary copes with all this craziness and misunderstanding.

He was out of his mind. *Mk 3:20-21*

Ordinary Time Week 3: Monday

There is evil in life, whatever title we want to give it, but it often comes through the human heart - from people.

Some say the devil of to-day is violence, and commentators say we can cope with it in one of two ways: on the one hand, we can have more laws and more prisons, or, on the other hand, we can work towards more caring homes and neighbourhoods.

President Kennedy's great words, 'Ask not what your country can do for you, but what can you do for your country,' are relevant.

An unclean spirit is in him. *Mk 3:22-30*

Ordinary Time Week 3: Tuesday

In her twenties, Patricia became totally paralysed. She lived in an iron lung which enabled her to breathe. Only her head was visible. She had beautiful long hair. We became good friends. She learned to work a typewriter, using her lips only. I asked her to write about life in an iron lung. I often read her thoughts.

She says, 'I don't adjust to being disabled easily. In my sleep and dreams, I'm still a mountain climber. Each day I wake I have to ajust again, and so waking is not my best time. Yet the day is full of little joys. There's no time for self-pity. Of course, there are times I would love to be able to wash my own face, and put on some make-up and get a new hair-do and spend the day in town getting some fabulous new clothes. Yet I don't fret or consider myself useless, because I do believe that God had a reason, 'a purpose' in allowing polio to hit me so hard.'

Anyone who does the will of God ... is my ... sister. *Mk 3:31-35*

Ordinary Time Week 3: Wednesday

This story consoles me because it says that the seed of God's love is constant, reliable, and mysteriously wonderful. His love is thrown recklessly and with abundance into the highways and by-ways, thorns and thistles, of human hearts. But there is such variety in the openess of human beings. Some of us are marginal, others give twenty, thirty or a hundred per cent. Who can judge?

This makes me think there has to be a lot of 'à la carte' Christianity as long as human beings are human. There is a danger in wanting to fit people into compartments, making them all the same. This does not seem to be God's way. He does the most surprising things, and maybe we'd be better to say 'How interesting!' rather than 'How terrible!'

Some fell in the wayside. Some fell among thorns ... *Mk 4:1-20*

Ordinary Time Week 3: Thursday

We lit a candle at the baby's baptism. We said, 'May this little child be a light of joy to you and to our world.'

We have great capacity for joy, both to experience it and to give it. It is one of the tests of Christianity: is there joy?

I know a priest who invites his Sunday congregation to 'Look baptised, and smile.'

Put your lamp on a lampstand to give light . *Mk 4:21-25*

Ordinary Time Week 3: Friday

Pope Paul VI made the extraordinary statement, that the reason for fall-away Christians was that the language of presenting Jesus' message was out of date. The good news is dressed in old dull clothes. It has become unintelligible. People are badly undernourished. Catechism answers and lists of rules alone are not the full good news. The false god of fear and judgement, that makes unhealthy guilt, is not good news.

The good news is that God loves us first. All life is gift. I am worthwhile because God is good. 'I am with you always.' To communicate this life-giving message, which humanises, is a great mission.

He spoke to them so far as they were capable of understanding
Mk 4:26-34

Ordinary Time Week 3: Saturday

Mick O'Connell was a great Kerry footballer. He won all the highest honours. He married Rosaleen. They had a baby, whose name was Diarmuid. He was handicapped with Downs Syndrome. Mick and Rosaleen felt shattered. Hopes of Diarmuid being a footballer, wearing the county jersey, were dashed.

Now, sixteen years later, Mick spoke to the press. He said, 'This boy is the joy of my life. I thought I knew what happiness was, but not really. This boy is happiness. I am caressed and loved and welcomed with hugs and smiles of friendship. This is real joy.'

Getting through the blows of sadness, disappointment, set-backs, death, goes on all the time, through the power of Jesus Christ.

Master, do you not care? We are going down! *Mk 4:35-41*

Ordinary Time Week 4: Monday

The film 'Prince of Tides' tells about a young man who was torn apart by the bad experience of childhood. The whole family was horrifically abused by intruders one night. The family decided to keep total silence about this terrible ordeal.Unspoken anger, built up into unspeakable hurt and cancerous bitterness that infected his marriage and his relationships. Visiting his sister in a mental home brings him in touch with a lady psychiatrist. She gives him professional and caring attention and becomes his saviour. He eventually breaks down and reveals his secret. He had never cried. Now he cries and cries. Talking and telling, he said, was more painful than the actual rape of years ago.

Love is the great healer that can take us our of our tombs, break the padlock of resentment, draw the poison, and unveil the family's hurt. He was restored to a new life with his wife and children. It was a resurrection.

The man lived in the tombs. *Mk 51:20*

Ordinary Time Week 4: Tuesday

It might seem strange to say that Jesus had an eye for women. He certainly had in today's story. There were two women in dire straits.

The woman with the blood problem is the more exciting story for me. A woman with a blood problem would be regarded as ritually unclean, according to the law, and would be excluded from the Temple and cut off from society. It would be strictly forbidden for her to touch a man's robe. So she had to hide in the crowd and not be caught.

Jesus could not tolerate this crushing belittling of a human person. He came to give life, meaning respect for the dignity and preciousness of a human person. He was forced to challenge the system. This kind of thinking had to be confronted. Jesus affirms life.

My daughter go in peace. Be free of your complaint. *Mk 5:21-43*

Ordinary Time Week 4: Wednesday

It is said that human beings are like flowers - they open up with the sun of love and rays of friendship. We are encouraged to grow through the love we experience. The mystery of life is that many are deprived of this love, with all kinds of sad results: possessiveness, restlessness, fears, money–obsession.

I rarely got a word of praise in my seminary days and I felt nervous for years afterwards as a priest. But through the love of people and the smiles of children, it began to dawn on me that I had some gifts and talents.

Jesus felt the pain of being underestimated and criticised, but he kept going in his Father's name.

He could work no miracle there. *Mk 6:1-6*

Ordinary Time Week 4: Thursday

God invites us, rather than forces us. Jesus was always inviting people to look at life in a new way: 'Look, God is Our Father. Why all the worry and overstress? He has loved us into life. He has fantastic plans for us.'

Be caring and kind to one another. Sometimes it is hard enough, but God Our Father helps us to get on together. Look at his wonderful world - every single little bird is a miracle, every blade of grass, every drop of water. We need to re-examine our thinking and our attitudes. That is the meaning of repentance.

True repentance feels drawn to God; false repentance feels driven by God.

They set off to preach repentance. *Mk 6:7-13*

Ordinary Time Week 4: Friday

A young man of nineteen wanted to ask religious questions. 'I'm into studying religion. I'm trying to find my way,' he said. 'Did Jesus have brothers and sisters? Were Adam and Eve giants? Did Noah live two hundred years?' I said, 'If Jesus had brothers or sisters, what difference does that make to life?' 'None, I suppose,' he said.

You see religion is about living life. One can prove anything out of the Bible. Anyhow, it is all summed up in one sentence: 'God loves us despite all our failings.' People always kept asking Jesus the wrong questions. We can be curious and superstitious. Sometimes we like to stay on the fringe. Instead of steering in the centre of the river, we're constantly attracted to the rocky edges and distractions. Jesus says, 'God is Father. People are first, before churches, before Bibles, before religious practices. Care for one another. Make our world of everyday a better world.'

Meanwhile, King Herod had heard about Jesus. *Mk 6:14-29*

Ordinary Time Week 4: Saturday

A Romanian baby was christened yesterday. I hope she will hear the story of Alexander Torea one day. He spent years in prison in Romania. He had a great sense of humour. He said, 'They have destroyed our churches, but we have made chapels out of the prisons.' The heart was his chapel, where faith and God were carried.

We face a lot of pressures in life, rearing children into teens, worry about work, drink, drugs, sickness. We feel trapped in an over-indulgent roundabout. There is no escape from living with people and the world around us, Jesus says. How to cope is the question. And one answer may be to make the heart a chapel.Make for yourself a moment of silence or prayer to the God within, whether for a moment on a bus, or a prayer before bed, or a prayer with the little ones.

Come away to some lonely place, all by yourselves, and rest a while. *Mk 6:30-34*

Ordinary Time Week 5: Monday

We've become more aware of the healing power of touch. We say, 'Keep in touch,' or 'I'll put you in touch with so and so.' And then we have aromatherapy and reflexology and so on. Jesus was a master of touch, and his touch brought harmony to the heart and harmony with others.

The sacraments are about touching each other and being touched by God. People welcome and support new life in baptism, care for their neighbours in the Sacrament of the Sick, and together celebrate the gift of life in memory of Jesus at Mass.

And all there who touched him were cured. *Mk 6:53-56*

Ordinary Time Week 5: Tuesday

There was once a saintly monk. People flocked to him for a cure. He always had a cat beside him. When he died people used still call to see the man with the cat. As time went on people forgot about the man and were looking for the holy cat. That is a temptation the good Lord warns about and tries to help us avoid. He is always directing our attention to caring for the other person – to the human needs and concerns – carrying and bearing others' burdens. He even says what we do to another we do to him. The roll call in Heaven will be about cups of tea given, smiles exchanged, helping hands, encouraging words. Fast he says, is not about, making me feel bad, but making others feel good. Blessing a mother after child birth is a 'thank you' not a purification rite. The Sabbath is not a rod to frighten us but an opportunity to enliven us about God's love, that makes our worth.

'Why do your disciples eat food... with unclean hands?' *Mk 7:1-13*

Ordinary Time Week 5: Wednesday

I was thinking about my friend Patricia who was totally paralysed in her early twenties. With a special typing machine, she was able to put her thoughts on paper. She writes: 'After being indoors all winter the first trip into fresh air is intoxicating. The smell and taste of air is like champagne and, as it wafts about your face, you can feel winter cobwebs lift away from your mind and all kinds of new ideas and schemes come rushing in.'

She writes about being fed, when one is unable to feed oneself. Being fed is never the same as feeding oneself. The food never tastes as good. Every nurse feeds you according to her own likes and dislikes. Sometimes the nicest bites are left on the plate. Being able to see your own food, and picking and choosing it, is half the pleasure of eating. When you can't see it, you get bored quite quickly, and anything you drink through a straw you can hardly taste at all.

Her inner beauty transformed the everyday challenges and touched people with joy.

Nothing that goes into a person from outside can make him unclean – it is from within. *Mk 7:14-23*

Ordinary Time Week 5: Thursday

He had and eye for scraps - scraps of food and scraps of humanity. A man at the rubbish dump was very surprised at the piles of good scraps – beautifully bound books, second hand T.Vs, shattered mirrors, a glistening saxaphone that made its last sound as it landed among rubbish cans. The Lord draws attention to the scraps and scrapes of living life – running the house, carrying shopping bags, holding children's hands; words of 'Thank you' 'That is nice' 'You are very good.' All the goings on of human beings are precious scraps in God's providence, part of the jigsaw of his caring graciousness that pervades our lives every second of every day.

'For saying this you may go home happy.' *Mk 7:24–30*

Ordinary Time Week 5: Friday

It often strikes me during a baptism, that we spend a lot of time looking in the wrong places for miracles. Just think about the miracle of speech, that comes as gift to that little baby in its mother's arms. And then there's the wondrous gift of hearing, and the two are related. Baptism celebrates both.

May the Lord be blessed in all our hearing.

May the Lord touch our lips with words

and songs of praise

for wonders beyond wonders.

They brought him a deaf man who had an impediment in his speech. *Mk 7:31-37*

Ordinary Time Week 5: Saturday

There are different kinds of hunger. The hunger to feel noticed, wanted or important, aches very deep and cannot be satisfied by bread alone. I smile at the delight of Adam when he was introduced to his wife. This new companion leaves him breathless. He is lost in extravagant words, 'Oh bone of my bone, flesh of my flesh.' Then, on the next page, he is grumpy with God, giving out about 'this woman you gave me.' It's the same person, but he doesn't even call her by name.

Where do we go wrong in our relationships? Marriage counsellors have no illusions about love growing cold. Love is a fragile gift, a flower that needs the sun to open. The sun it needs includes doing jobs together, respecting talent, shouldering weakness, saying, 'Sorry. I didn't mean it. Let us start again.' Loving another has to be worked at if it is to yield fruit.

I feel sorry for the people. *Mk 8:1-10*

Ordinary Time Week 6: Monday

A man told me that he never reads lives of the saints because the real saints never make it into the top twenty. The real saints are the ordinary everyday people who get meals, mind the children, make a living, and bear the disappointments and sufferings of life. The nurse said to me, 'There is a temptation to be preoccupied with the dramatics in nursing – controlling life and death machines or techniques of resuscitation. We may miss the uneventful, like a cup of tea for anxious relatives, easing anxiety, wheeling people around – just being there.

Jesus was too human and practical to waste time on discussions. The signs of God are all around, in us, beside us, not in dramatics.

No sign shall be given – he went to the opposite shore. *Mk 8:11-13*

Ordinary Time Week 6: Tuesday

The professor was trying to explain the theology of miracles to a dull student. All his best efforts were of no avail. He invited the student to stand up. He gave him a kick in the backside, saying, 'Did you feel that?' The baffled student said, 'Yes, I did.' 'Well now, it would be a miracle if you didn't feel it!'

The frustration and humanity of Christ in today's story is very consoling for any parent, teacher, leader or priest. His words, 'Do you not understand? Are your minds closed? Do you not remember? Have you no eyes? Have you no ears?'

How we long to put old heads of wisdom and understanding on young shoulders, and it doesn't work. God is a waiting God. He waits for us too. We do what we can, and we wait in hope.

Do you not understand? *Mk 8:14-21*

Ordinary Time Week 6: Wednesday

We live life at home, not in chapels or Churches. Church helps us to appreciate the God of home and ordinary experiences. Trying to see life this way is *faith.*. God is Father of all, a pervasive providence in the scraps and scrapes of everyday living and working.

Jesus helps a man to see, and then he sends him home. It is there, at home, that we have to put our insight, our energy, our joy to good account first. I have 'mea culpa' memories of being labelled a street angel but a home devil.

Jesus sent him home. *Mk 8:22-26*

Ordinary Time Week 6: Thursday

A vicious scorpion was dangling from a branch over-hanging a fast flowing river. An old man took pity on the scorpion which was falling to its death and went to the rescue. As he brought the scorpion to safety, he received a vicious bite from the frightened creature. The old man cried out in pain. A young man who watched the whole drama shouted, 'You stupid old fool, why did you bother with that scorpion? Didn't you know he would sting?' The old man said, 'If it is my way to want to save and suffer pain in the process, why should you call me stupid? Why should I change?'

It was Jesus's way to love and to save, to give value to human creatures, but it involved pain, opposition even death. Peter thought it was stupid having to suffer, but Jesus was teaching Peter the meaning of love. Love cannot be real love without pain.

Peter started to remonstrate with him. *Mk 8:27-33*

Ordinary Time Week 6: Friday

'The business is doing fine. Home and family are well. But I was happier when I had nothing,' John said. He explained that his problem was not about money or health. It was a jealous streak in his make-up. 'I know that my attitude is wrong towards my wife. It is unreasonable because loving someone does not mean owning someone. But it is there like a chain holding and haunting me.'

His words prompted me to ask, 'How does one find oneself in life?' Jesus says this is the most basic of questions. He says life flowers not so much by gathering up as by giving away or giving way. The heart grows bigger the more it gives away, it is said. Loving is built into our make up and jealousy is a threat to loving. Perhaps we are called to new ways of loving, making more time to be together with our loved ones. Business and the chores of life can over pre-occupy us. We need to acknowledge and refresh our loving relationship with talks and walks and small celebrations together.

Anyone who loses his life for my sake will save it. *Mk 8:35*

Ordinary Time Week 6: Saturday

When I think of happiness I think of Maggie. Maggie has spent most of her life in a hospital for mildly mentally handicapped girls. She is now almost blind. She waits at the door to greet me every Monday morning. It is a great start to the week. She takes me by the hand and says, 'Oh you're very cold. You must have a nice cup of hot tea.' She inquires about the sick people I've confided to her prayers. When I ask about her well-being, she tells me about the lovely tea she had in a friend's house. When I ask did she take a little drink, she rocks with laughter and begins to sing, 'Show Me the Way to Go Home'. She tells me about her friend who is ill or an acquaintance that has died, and then she sings, 'Pack up your troubles in your old kit bag and smile, smile, smile,' and does a little dance. What is Maggie's secret of happiness?

I think she is saying that there is no happiness without struggle and pain. Mothers and parents know this. There is a tension in our human make-up. We have a foot in earth and a foot in heaven because of our dreams, wishes and desires. Maggie can keep the balance right because of her private chats with God. The chapel of the heart travels with us all the time. We don't have to go to special places or shrines. If we do, it is to become more aware that the ordinary is extraordinary. Happiness is God-given and self-made.

Rabbi, it is wonderful to be here. *Mk 9:2-13*

Ordinary Time Week 7: Monday

I heard about 'Books on Wheels' yesterday. The idea is to make books available to shut-in people who are not very mobile. It works rather like meals on wheels. Those who were receiving this service said that it was a new lease of life, like the joy and consolation of a friend. For the weak-sighted there were large-print books. There were also Tape Books.

Everyday miracles are made by people for people. The deaf hear, the blind see, the dumb speak.

My son, there is a Spirit of dumbness in him. *Mk 9:14-29*

Ordinary Time Week 7: Tuesday

The singer Christy Moore says that he sees the same things in life, but differently now. Life is better. There is not the need in him now to spend long hours of night socialising and absorbed by people.

God is very gracious in the way he waits for us. Parents worry about Mass-going on Sunday. God waits on our growing and knows that we don't understand yet. It is not fair to be blaming parents or priest. The Mass calls for participation together in all that makes up life. 'What does God do for us at Mass?' is a good question.

They did not understand and were afraid to ask. *Mk 9:30-37*

Ordinary Time Week 7: Wednesday

'Begrudging' is a word we hear often. What does it mean? We can't wish another person well or be glad for them. We think of their flaw or fault first. A begrudging person can't think 'thanks' first, but thinks, 'Why haven't we a heated swimming pool in the parish?' It is a kind of a sickness that sees the cup always half empty instead of half full.

Trying to follow Christ is the opposite stance. Rejoice with those that rejoice. Be sad with those who are sad. Try to be in the other person's shoes. Whenever there is good done, healing present, or joy expressed, it is God's blessing. Let us be happy for the blessing and try to share in its enjoyment.

He was not one of us. We tried to stop him. You must not.
Mk 9:38-40

Ordinary Time Week 7: Thursday

How gifted we are. We have hearts and hands, feet and eyes. Try buying any of those blessings. God asks us to be life-givers. You have been life-givers today in many ways: meals prepared and served, children got ready for school. There are visits, smiles, welcomes, instructions.

We are aware too that we can use our gifts to hurt, to let someone down, to play false, to cheat. This makes us feel mean. There are secrets of darkness in all of us, but they are more than balanced by blessings of light. We can do so much to make our world a better world, to up-lift people, to be life givers.

A cup of water in my name will not lose reward.   *Mk 9:41-50*

Ordinary Time Week 7: Friday

There is a song about 'Leaving'. It should be a marriage song. She complained, 'He never left his mother and home. Still Mammy's boy.' He complained, 'The mother-in-law might as well be living with us.' She said, 'He can't leave his work. He even has a computer in bed with him.' He said, 'She can't leave the children to be themselves. 24 hours a day for twenty years with children is bad for them and bad for us.' She says, 'He can't leave his mates, the pub, or football.' This leaving is some challenge. It is a must in order to grow more human. Jesus is an expert in leaving.

A man must leave his father and mother. *Mk 10:1-12*

Ordinary Time Week 7: Saturday

I often wonder how Jesus would cope with children 'on their own' at Mass. In his day, the people were with the children, bringing them to Jesus. That was easier. I have found children very reasonable and easy to please at Mass. Would the good Lord expect children to do nothing, say nothing, see nothing, understand nothing at Mass, just sit and be quiet?

There is a lot to interest children in a wholesome way at Mass, but adults and priests must work together. While we wait, it is always helpful to acknowledge the presence of children by asking to 'see their hands.' At the beginning of Mass, we pray together with our hands. Raising two hands for the 'Let us give thanks' is appreciated and a clap at the 'Holy Holy' makes their day. Shaking hands is real for children. So, while we await the participation, singing and drama, prayers and readings, I am grateful for the hands of children.

The people were bringing the children to Jesus. *Mk 10:13-16*

Ordinary Time Week 8: Monday

'He'll leave it all behind him,' people say and they won't even remember or say a prayer - that's money. It is difficult to have balance. We can only wear one suit at a time, eat one meal at a time. Greed is a run-away horse.

There is no commandment that tells us how exactly to spend our money. Money is the 'bread' and staff of life.

'Give to the poor,' Jesus says. It is good for us and good for them. The poor have a thousand faces, beginning with our own family and reaching to lives that are dull without hope. Our Mass is always a challenge to give to the poor. We can be irritated by the calls and reminders of generosity, but they are blessed opportunities too. Asking for money to help others is practical Christianity. Sitting down to plan money matters for to-day's living and tomorrow's departure is worthwhile.

He was a man of great wealth.   *Mk 10:17-27*

Ordinary Time Week 8: Tuesday

Gabrielle Bossis is a modern day saint. She finds God in the street, in her travels, in the rush of life. She finds God in wealth. She says to God, 'I'll buy clothes to adorn the Altar.' God says, 'No. Make them with your own hands.' It can be easier to buy, but more loving to make. Putting oneself into a gift gives greater joy.

I admire people who put thought, time and imagination into gifts for others and into celebrations. A card of thanks from a little child with its own hand writing, colour and decorations is a real masterpiece.

Repaid a hundred times over.   *Mk 10:28-31*

Ordinary Time Week 8: Wednesday

When we are sick, we are not able to pray in the ordinary way. We have to wait. We go from being active, able to do for ourselves, to being passive, dependent on others. We are in the hands of others. This waiting pain is called sharing the passion of Jesus. So the Mass always remembers the sick.

Have mercy on us, O Lord, and look on us.
Let your compassion hasten to meet us.
We are in the depths of distress.
O God our Saviour, come to help us.
Forgive us our sins.
Rescue us for the sake of your name.
Let the groans of prisoners come before you. *Ps 78*

Ordinary Time Week 8: Thursday

The film *Dancing with Wolves* was powerful. John Dunbarr goes west to explore new frontiers, away from the madness of war. He meets up with an Indian tribe. They have great fear and suspicion of the white man. But he is a peacemaker with people and nature. A wolf becomes his best friend. His patience wins out. He is accepted into the tribe by the leader. Names are exchanged. He is clothed in Indian dress. They are a people who live in harmony with themselves and nature. He is accepted as a good human being. However, the war mongers catch up with him, his own people. They arrest him, torture him and try to kill him as a traitor.

A powerful image of Christ! He came and died to bring harmony to people, to help us to live at peace with one another and with our environment.

Courage, he is calling. *Mk 10:46-52*

Ordinary Time Week 8: Friday

A man phoned into the radio yesterday complaining, 'Why do Christian people have a pre-occupation with flames and hell? This is an insult to God. Why would Our Lady of Fatima talk to a little girl of ten years about flames? It is extraordinary,' he said, 'to hear such words when God describes himself as love and Jesus' constant teaching is of the loving Father who never changes his love for us, with our warts and all.'

'The Lord takes delight in his people,' the prayer says. 'The birds that sing for us say, 'The Lord takes delight in his people.' Why did Jesus put people out of the Temple? They misunderstood God. They wanted to put God in their own pocket, use him to their advantage. But God always roams free – a God of surprises who can't be reserved. All are his favourites.

My home ... for all peoples. *Mk 11:11-26*

Ordinary Time Week 8: Saturday

Christopher Nolan has been called the greatest person of our times. He lived in a world of silence, totally handicapped, except for his mind. Through the extraordinary dedication of his parents he learned to express himself in writing poems. He is one of the great writers of this century.

He says the changing point in his life came when he accused his mother of bringing him into this life as a cripple.

His mother sat him down and said 'Look, I did not pray to have you a cripple. You have a mind. You can think, you can see, and we accept and love you as you are.' I think this is the kind of 'authority' that Christ preaches. It is an authority that makes the other person feel worthwhile and of value. He made people feel good and the overflow was to make others feel good. Authority that accepts and loves us as we are, not for our success or what we do, is surely God-like.

'I will tell you my authority.' *Mark 11:27-33*

Ordinary Time Week 9: Monday

Mary experienced great poverty and deprivation in her work in a shanty town in Africa. Home on holidays, she went to Mass with her sister who was a single girl, well employed. When the collection plate came around, the young girl put a few pennies on the plate. Her sister spoke to her afterwards and said, 'You know there is a worse disease than cancer, and it is greed.'

There is an old saying: 'The more we have the more we want.' The opportunity of being asked to give is a way of avoiding greed. We all use excuses for not giving. 'They're well-off enough.' 'The State should pay for these things.' 'They misuse the money.'

If we have no God to believe in, the danger is we make a God out of ourselves and that is pretty stupid and disastrous.

They sent him away empty handed. *Mk 12:1-12*

Ordinary Time Week 9: Tuesday

I listened to a good woman reflecting on the happenings of today. We get no vocations. Our houses are closing. We try to make provisions for our elderly and sick. There are lots of meetings and gatherings, goings and comings. I'm sure there is good in all. But she said, 'Nobody can really tell you what to do. One has to work it out for oneself and 'do' oneself.' She personally, in her mature years, would like simply being with ordinary people in a parish setting.

I don't want to be organising people, or being left with responsibilities at my age, or telling what to do. I like being with mothers in the creche, being at the bingo, standing around the Church admiring the young, travelling on the bus. I like a stand and wait mission - a presence, wherever there are people.

When Jesus was asked for answers he didn't give the simple answers – maybe because there are no simple answers. He gave a reply and the gist of it was, 'You've got to work it out for yourself in good conscience.' *Mk 12:13-17*

Ordinary Time Week 9: Wednesday

I had an aunt whose name was Sister Raphael. She lived in Belfast. I went to visit her when I was studying for the priesthood. She was old. She said two things to me that I remember. 'Stop frowning. It makes you look old and serious. You should be bright and out-going and if ever you are a chaplain to Sisters, don't waste time fustering in the sacristy before you start Mass, keeping everybody waiting and frozen in Church.'

Raphael is another name for 'God heals'. He comes to our aid when we ask his help to heal our minds in depression, to heal our hearts in marriage and sickness. His healing messengers are very often people and services around us - his hands. Jesus says, 'We can give life to the living. We trust our dead to the Lord.'

I am the God of Abraham, the God of Isaac and the God of Jacob. *Mk 12:18-27*

Ordinary Time Week 9: Thursday

The radio said yesterday that Japanese women live longer than Irish women. The commentator said that Irish women lack balance in caring for self and are over-absorbed in family and children. They have no life of their own. It is said that marriage is like the separate strings of a guitar. Each string is separate, different, unique. When they choose to come together they make good sound.

We cannot be possessed by anybody or anything. Each person is special, precious, unique. A healthy self-image is desirable, and so is a good education. I believe that Christ had a healthy self-image, a concern for self that desires privacy and a feeling of being loved - an intimacy with God and a concern for others that pushed him into caring sacrifices.

You must love your neighbour as yourself. *Mk 12:25-34*

Ordinary Time Week 9: Friday

I met a little boy going to play school. He said 'Hello Father Hick-ey.' I shook hands with him. He said 'You're great. ' The words kept ringing in my ears. Somehow I needed to hear those words on Monday morning. The people hear Christ's words with delight. He must really have made them feel great. This is the challenge of Faith that believes God is love. He thinks we are great.

God praises us first and foremost, otherwise we would not be here. He says 'you are great.' But we won't believe. It is too good to be true. We prefer to think that he is telling us our faults first, and about his annoyance. It is not easy to believe that God loves us without condition, without 'ifs.' Telling people their faults rarely brings change in life or marriage or work-place. It is non product-ive. Preoccupation with sin, devils, guilt, evil is not healthy - I must meet this little boy more often.

'The people heard – with delight. *Mk 12:35-37*

Ordinary Time Week 9: Saturday

A widow said that she was most consoled by Cardinal Ó Fiaich, who gave her a hug and said, 'I'd be shattered too.' Christ had great heart for the widow. His best stories are about widows. His mother was a widow. He knew the story inside out.

Having a heart for a person is more important than having money. The heart makes time for a call, a chat. The heart listens and does not offer answers. The heart invites out to please another person, not just to fulfil an obligation.

A poor widow put in two small coins. *Mk 12:38-44*

Ordinary Time Week 10: Monday

Would I help her to trace her mother, Mary asked. 'I'm an orphan-age child. I had a baby at 17 years. I could not offer the baby the life he deserved. I had him adopted to a good family. I made one pro-viso: if ever he wanted to contact me, I'd be happy to meet him. I eventually married, but we cannot have any children. I feel very lonely at times, especially at Christmas, birthdays and celebra-tions. I feel that I have no one. I belong to no one.

Mary is my woman of the beatitudes.

How happy are the poor in spirit. *Mk 5:1-12*

Ordinary Time Week 10: Tuesday

We were saddened when a row of young trees was vandalised around our homes. The trees breathe the same air and are caressed by the same sun as ourselves. They put on different clothes and colour through the seasons. They welcome us. They delight us. They give us promise of encouragement, hope, renewal. We are all sustained by Mother Earth.

Our bereavement was softened by a man of exceptional thoughtfulness. He decided to bandage the broken tree limbs and raise up the drooped heads. He said that it happened to an apple tree in his garden once. 'I bandaged it and the tree gave me two hundred apples that year. Some may be gone beyond repair, but at least they'd have a look of dignity.'

Grace abounds. Better to light a candle than curse the darkness. Weakness of character, darkness, tragedy, we always have with us. But the life-giving attitude that lifts the weak, shoulders a burden with others, puts out the hand, looks up with hope, is surely God in action.

Seeing your good works they praise the Father.   *Mt 5:13-16*

Ordinary Time Week 10: Wednesday

A writer said that his joy and weakness was the taste of strawberries. Taste is magic. I'm not supposed to eat chocolate, but I sneak a bar an odd time. I don't gulp. I really savour, caress that taste. The first refreshing drink when one is thirsty is a deeply satisfying taste.

Yesterday, an elderly lady was waiting beside me to have her arm x-rayed in the Casualty Dept. We got talking. 'Don't think I fell because of drink,' she said, 'I do drink and I love it. You know,' she said, 'the best drink is brandy and put scalding water in it with sugar.' We laughed and rejoiced at the thoughts of 'taste', a good preparation for hospital visits.

Show me the path of life, The fullness of joy... *Ps 15:4*

Ordinary Time Week 10: Thursday

How to cope with hate? People who have experienced the hate of being tortured in prison tell us that unless one tries to forgive, even have sympathy for the torturer, the hate infects oneself like a kind of possession.

Jesus says, 'Forgive enemies. That is the way to be more human and at peace.' Best for yourself.

A religious Sister was deeply hurt by the Superior because she felt that she was treated unjustly. She could not sleep with feelings of hate. A friend said to her, 'Throw out that rubbish that's weighing you down.' She protested, 'I'm not able.' The friend advised her to pray the Our Father in moments of hurtful hate feelings and take it slowly. Sleep and peace did come.

Your brother has something against you. Go first … *Mt 5:20-26*

Ordinary Time Week 10: Friday

Most of us have plants in jars and pots at home. Some people say that they talk to plants. Paul would say, 'Let the plant talk to you.' The plant says, 'I have mysterious power within me, wherever it comes from. I've been uprooted and changed around a lot in my life, but I've never despaired. I've been knocked down by the wind and ways of the world but never knocked out. There is a kind of death in my body when I'm blooming, so death is at work, and life too.'

We are the plants embedded in Christ, jars that hold treasures.

We are earthenware jars that hold treasure. *2 Cor 4:7-15*

Ordinary Time Week 10: Saturday

The Psychologist and Psychiatrist highlight the wonder and mystery of our human make up. They see into our dreams, our romances, our affairs, our staying young and growing old and our grieving, our celebrating, our words.We regret words we did not say to our loved ones. Anne said to me. 'I accept the bad news of my terminal illness. It gives me time to say my 'hello's' and 'goodbyes.' Why should God put the clock back for me. And the way we use words is important. In marriage the Counsellor advised that instead of telling the husband that he had smelly feet it is better to say 'I am a bit odd and strange and smells put me right off, would you wash the 'ould feet for me.' Caring attention with words can make a big difference. That kind of attention someone called 'repentance.' Caring attention and sensitivity with words is Christ's way and makes a better world.

'All you need to say is 'yes' if you mean yes.'   *Mt 5: 33-37*

Ordinary Time Week 11: Monday

My little nephew got an attack of croup. He was frightened and asked his mother to get the doctor and say some prayers. The crisis passed and his mother said, 'Don't forget to thank God for making you better.' He said, 'He didn't make me better until the doctor gave me the injection first.' We are God's fellow-workers.

As God's fellow-workers, don't reject grace received. *Mt 5:33-37*

Ordinary Time Week 11: Tuesday

The king asked the Street Artist to paint a picture of the Last Supper. The King and all his household assembled in the Great Hall of the Palace on exhibition day. As the poor artist unveiled his coloured masterpiece, the King looked shocked and angry. In the painting, the artist included not just Jesus and the twelve apostles, but all kinds of people, even dogs and animals. Some looked sad, sick, depressed, angry; others looked joyful and happy. The King shouted at the Artist, 'Of what is this a painting?' 'My Lord,' the artist said, 'This is a painting of God our Father who makes the sun shine on good and bad, makes the rain fall on honest and dishonest. That's my idea of the Last Supper.'

He sends his rain on bad men as well as good. Mt 5:43-48

Ordinary Time Week 11: Wednesday

We celebrated a first birthday last night of 'Baptism Friends' in the parish. There was tea and wine and goodies. The little room was festooned with colour photos of babies and families. Posters on the wall said, 'Baptism Friends make friendship in the community'. We recalled that baptism is about friendship, God's friendship loving us into life, our friendship with one another. Little gifts and visits to the newly arrived help us to touch and notice one another. Stories are told of meeting parents and babies in shops, at bus stops, at Mass. Smiles are exchanged, caring enquiries are made. It is good to celebrate the seeds of friendship that grow abundantly around us, that soften and soothe the journey through life.

When you fast, put oil on your head and wash your face.

Mt 6:1-6, 16-18

Ordinary Time Week 11: Thursday

I like re-visiting a scene or place of younger days, an old house, a football field, a river, a Church, a font, a cemetery. Somehow it says more now. A lady who had a bad accident told me the same about her prayers. 'I just sat in Church one day and said a familiar prayer that I learned in my childhood. It never struck me before, the power and strength in the words. The words spoke new life and hope to me. I was refreshed and felt grateful.'

The master prayer taught by Jesus is the Our Father. Somehow it gets the angle on God and life, on the world and our needs in right perspective. Alright to sing and say together joyfully, but important too to take time to sift the real gold, word by word, in a quiet moment.

Do not babble using many words. Pray 'Our Father.' *Mt 6:7-15*

Ordinary Time Week 11: Friday

Twenty-one years ago, I was helping a family to adopt a baby. It was complex. The Sister was extraordinarily helpful and really put her heart and mind into bringing happiness. I wrote a card of thanks saying, 'You are the best thing that happened to me this year.'

I had long since forgotten the card, but not the person. That person bumped into me last week and said, 'Do you remember the card you sent? We all got great joy reading it.'

What is of lasting value? I think seeds of friendship that we scatter everyday, words of friendship that make us wonder-workers.

Store up treasures in heaven. *Mt 6:19-23*

Ordinary Time Week 11: Saturday

I was walking near Dublin Bay, mulling over the chores of life. Suddenly I was called to attention by enchanting sky music – a lark carolling in the heavens, so tiny I had difficulty sighting this musical genius; so high I marvelled how its sweet song could carry the waves of distance. That skylark sang its heart out for me. This one little bird was a natural orchestra, performing free.

Eventually, my song-friend descended to earth in five stages, perfect breath control at each level, poised suspended between heaven and earth, and then disappeared into the grassed sand dunes.

The best things in life are free. Everyday, God calls us to hope, even to be carefree. He invites us to look at the birds. I gave my songster a secret clap, hoping nobody noticed. I spoke for all our city and the surrounding bay, the distant Dublin mountains and the ever-changing white clouds in that blue sky.

Look at the birds in the sky. *Mt 6:24-34*

Ordinary Time Week 12: Monday

Thomas Merton said that God in his goodness hides our faults from ourselves. It would be too depressing if we saw them too much. It is better to think of what we can do than to think of what we don't do. Another great spiritual writer used to say, 'If we want to know our own failings, our specks and beams of blindness, check out what we criticise in others. Most likely that is our own problem.' People can often be critical of other people's children. Then, when they have children of their own, I've heard them say how insensitive and unhelpful people are to children at times like travelling, shopping, visiting, and indeed in the Church.

Why do you observe the splinter in the other's eye and never notice the plank in your own? *Mt 7:1-5*

Ordinary Time Week 12: Tuesday

How do we like to be treated in the shop, on the bus, driving the car? How do we like to be treated by family, neighbour, priest? How do we like to be treated when we're in love and happy, when we're afraid, worried, in pain or bereaved?

Treating others as we would like to be treated is the meaning of all the Laws and prophets, a powerful statement that humanises religion.

That is the meaning of the Law and the prophets. *Mt 7:12-14*

Ordinary Time Week 12: Wednesday

The Leaving Class got a special talk from the President of the College. This was a kind of pep-talk to prepare us for the bad and treacherous world that lay before us in a few months' time. I could never feel that the world was bad because I was playing on the college football team, hoping to play on parish and county teams, and I felt a special 'grá' for a girl in the nearby convent school.

Anyhow, the talk of the year went on behind closed doors, spoken with fear and trembling. There are two pitfalls to beware of: Punch and Judy. Punch is the drink and Judy is women. Even then, I couldn't think of life without Judy and Punch and I haven't changed my mind. Our good president was doing his best. Surely the God of Love is the God of wine and women? Punch and Judy and John and Mary.

You will be able to tell them by their fruits. *Mt 7:15-20*

Ordinary Time Week 12: Thursday

I like the story of Jonah. It spotlights God's thinking about us. Jonah talks to God alright, but he does not like God's style of chat back. 'Your people in Niniveh, God, are a rotten lot, no way can any good come from these.' Excuse me Jonah I am asking you 'Go.' So Jonah goes with a sour face, hoping for failure. It works the opposite way. God's mercy embarrasses. Because God thinks more of us than we think of ourselves. He is more than polite words that says 'Lord, Lord. He is the one who accepts us with failures, weaknesses and all. God asks 'Do you like that flower. I made it for you. Do you like you pet. I made it for you.' Jesus' idea of peace is generous too. It is not just sitting on the fence saying words. It is getting involved with the human and the earthy, the people and the problems, coping with moods, settling kitchen rows, helping others, the endless demands of daily living.

'It is not those who say Lord, Lord... those who do.' *Mt 7:21-29*

Ordinary Time Week 12: Friday

Peggy said 'my son mended that rosary beads. I'd be lost without that and the few prayers. But I fell asleep reading the Novena prayers.' I said to God 'If you want me cured you will cure me, and if you don't, you won't. I love to see you coming. You are marvellous.' When I returned the compliment she would say. 'You must be jokin.' She was truly marvellous. Life was tough. There was himself and the drink. But I stuck with it and I'm glad. The family is so good, I miss himself so much.

The family never left her bedside. All conversations were held around her bed. It was like sitting around the fire at home. There was no hush, hush of secrecy but a total openess and human warmth. Affection prompted the family even to lie in bed with Peggy. We are indeed touched with blessings of affection that spell the presence of our gracious God.

Jesus touched him... of course I went too. *Mt 8:1–4*

Ordinary Time Week 12: Saturday

When my father retired, he liked to go to 10 o'clock Mass, not so much for the devotion, I think, as for the friendship of seeing, meeting, talking to people and going to someone's house for a cup of tea. I don't think he would have liked tea-friendship with Mass. Many would say that this is an important emphasis today. I never believed that Mass was meant to be boring, even allowing for all our limitations and imperfections.

Worshipping God is earthed in caring for and noticing people. The morning Mass stories are very earthy. Jesus meets a soldier with a different religion. Jesus touches Peter's mother-in-law. He has words with the mentally disturbed. Abraham gives the tea of friendship to three strangers. Suddenly the three strangers become one person - the Lord.

He touched her hand. *Mt 8:5-17*

Ordinary Time Week 13: Monday

Sister Provincial explained that the Sisters would be leaving our parish. Sixty five per cent of all Sisters in the Order were in 65 age bracket. 'My work,' she explained, 'is providing a respite for retiring Sisters who have given their most on the missions and elswhere. How to provide for their needs with dignity and humanity with minimal salaries is very challenging.' She admitted that she herself would love to work with young people or with the sick in parish life, but her call now was in administration and negotiation - endless meetings, complaints, uncertainties, and dealing with banks and solicitors, buying and selling property.

I came away saddened, but with admiration too. Somehow, somewhere new doors are being opened and, if the bottom line of all religion is how we treat others, then new life is guaranteed.

Follow me and leave the dead to bury the dead. *Mt 8:18-22*

Ordinary Time Week 13: Tuesday

I went to Skellig Rock. There is a monastery ruin there which is a thousand years old, ten miles into the Atlantic off the coast of Kerry. What I remember most was the boat journey, the waves, the fear. The monks of long ago would really feel the great Psalm prayer: 'Out of the depths I cry to you, O Lord.'

The Lord is with us in the depths of fear, but he seems to be asleep. A fear that grabs everyone at some time is fear of death. Jesus rehearses death for us to-day. It is 'a crossing over' with Jesus to the order side. We don't send for the boat. It comes and takes us. Some boat journeys are long. Some are short. But for each it is complete.

He got into the boat first and was followed by his disciples.
Mt 8:23-27

Ordinary Time Week 13: Wednesday

I was chaplain for a time in a Mental Hospital. One day at Mass, I foolishly remarked that God wants us to accept our cross. A lady started shouting, saying, 'It is not God that has me here. It is my family. It is the doctors who put this cross on me – not God.'

We are people 'in the depths' at times, with pain, shame, or desperate loneliness. We are in the tombs of depression, torn apart, raw, wanting to scream.

Jesus's story says, 'He knows. He heals.' There is hope. Great signs of hope are the caring we see in hospitals, community, and most of all in families where depression is seen like any other illness. There is understanding and compassion.

The demoniacs came towards him out of the tombs.   *Mt 8:28-34*

Ordinary Time Week 13: Thursday

Getting up is easier when we have someone or something to look forward to. People in late life often say getting up is a 'Thank you for the blessing of another day.' Picking up the joy of the day is 'gold for heaven and the making of God's kingdom on earth,' – the cups of tea, chatting, planning, smiling, business dealing, shopping and schooling, playing, dancing and making up.

All in all, it adds up to coming home to be oneself, accepting the reality, the wonder and the mischief that is me and approaching others in all the ways that can make life good and make our world better. We are coming home to God as we get up, pick up and go home.

Get up, pick up, go off home. *Mt 9:1-8*

Ordinary Time Week 13: Friday

A teacher in school gave me this advice about religion. He said, 'Keep the ball on the ground and they can all touch it.' Simple, not fussy, not complicated, but easier said than done. I get bogged down and feel out of touch. I read of new places of pilgrimage, another vision of Mary. New prayer-exercises, new-style retreats. There are sabbaticals, live-ins, touch-ins, pray-ins, reflexology, meditation, contemplation. I am sure that all is blessing and the human person is an extraordinary variety in make-up. There is a place for everyone. Yet I wonder what the man in the pub having his pint would say?

God is where we are now, to-day. You mean now in beds and breakfasts. You mean now in worries, sickness, jobs, money, relationships. You mean now, talking to myself on the bus, saying Hail Marys, coping with depressing people, hoping for a laugh.

Tax Collectors and sinners came to sit at the table with Jesus and eat with him. *Mt 9:9-13*

Ordinary Time Week 13: Saturday

Brendan was young and successful in business when he died. He would say to me, 'Liam, I'm a quality man. In business I want the best for my customers and for my staff. I wear a quality suit, drive a dashy car, but I always come home to lunch in my overalls because the children might get the wrong impression.'

Work is important; you make your world. Christ is a quality man. He says, 'I'm like fresh wine.' Wine we associate with joy, love, festivity, satisfaction, togetherness. He says, 'I'm the bridegroom calling for celebration, making happiness. I'm a quality man. I'm fresh skinned like a smiling David, not wizened, half dead with the begrudging lifeless look.' Catch on to living – spread the news.

He is bridegroom. He is new wine. *Mt 9:14-17*

Ordinary Time Week 14: Monday

What is it that makes us feel good – a word of praise, a word of thanks, the acceptance that children give?

Christ certainly had the gift of making a person feel good. He would be in feminist causes for to-day's stories. Worse than the death of a young girl was the ritual death of a woman with a blood disorder. In her society she would be regarded as unclean, unfit, excluded from religious society. For her to touch the robe a man was wearing would be forbidden by law, so she had to hide in the crowd. Jesus broke the chains that were dragging her down and called her 'my daughter. You are beautiful. Have courage.' It was alright for men to shed their blood. This inhumanity Jesus challenged and purified. His Spirit breathes the same blessing on the joy of motherhood today.

Courage, my daughter. *Mt 9:18-26*

Ordinary Time Week 14: Tuesday

I liked the film *Babette's Feast*. Babette is gifted in making food dishes. She is forced to leave her restaurant in Paris because of the Revolution. She goes to Holland. She is given refuge by two pious ladies. She will cook for them. Seventeen years later she receives a surprise letter from Paris. She has won a lottery of ten thousand Francs. She asks a favour from the ladies. Allow her to give a dinner to the household, to the village and to friends. But it must be a French style dinner. Preparations began. Foods of all kinds and wines of the best were carted from Paris.

The ladies and some villagers got worried about this extravagence. They held a meeting. They would attend the dinner, but in a subdued, cautious mood. All arrived. The tables were beautifully laden. Food was served. As the night warmed up hearts softened, tongues loosened, old rows were resolved, people openly forgave each other. The night ended with all holding hands and singing together. Babette served all night and then expressed her total joy that the meal cost ten thousand francs, the exact amount that it would cost in her treasured Paris restaurant. This crazy kind of generosity hints at our God who releases, forgives, affirms and celebrates us even in this life.

Nothing like this has ever been seen in Israel. *Mt 9:32–38*

Ordinary Time Week 14: Wednesday

The lady said that she runs 'workshops', helping people to see the wonder of self. A good vision of the world begins with a good vision of self. We are gifted and wounded. Maybe we have overstressed the wounds. We underestimate self and our gifts.

Jesus gives authority to each one to-day. He singles out each, name by name. He builds up self-image, empowering us to be lifegiving. The Lady said that in the many challenges of life we can do three things: become aware of a need, an opportunity, a challenge; make a choice; then respond.

When we make a choice, it brings responsibility. This empowers oneself through the grace of God and is the making of a person.

These are the names – and he sent them out. *Mt 10:1-7*

Ordinary Time Week 14: Thursday

Archbishop Tutu, in South Africa, describes two pictures. In the first, we see people all in white with palm branches, processing with serious faces towards a light in the sky. In the second, people are laughing, dancing, singing, playing cards. The second, he says, is our real God. Jesus was always splendidly affirming life. We blossom in the presence of people who see the good in us and who can coax the best out of us. We wither and wilt in the presence of people always finding fault with us. Jesus saw the quality of Mary Magdalen that nobody else noticed. Others saw loose living. He saw generosity of heart.

An old football coach used to say to us before a game, even when we felt we were facing giants, 'Ye have it in ye, lads. Show them.' Life-giving words.

Cure - Raise - Cleanse - Give. *Mt 10:7-15*

Ordinary Time Week 14: Friday

Playing for God's kingdom demands waiting and tactics. Jesus says, 'I am an ambassador of God's spirit to the people that surround me everyday, to the world I live in.' We are challenged constantly to wait for people to grow in God's good time. Our children don't see life as we do. We can't put an old head on young shoulders. They opt out of religious habits and practices, but are good at heart. They get involved with strange people.

We forget to say 'thanks' for help through the years. We feel that nobody wants to care or know. We need patience and tactics. Jesus promises us his Spirit. It will be given you what to say.

What you are to say will be given you when the time comes.
Mt 10:16-23

Ordinary Time Week 14: Saturday

I used to worry, 'What will I say if I'm asked an awkward religious question?' Going to work in a parish in London increased my anxiety. People often ask, 'But what will I say?' I feel that Jesus' friends were pestering him with 'What will we say?' questions. He explains that that is not important. What is important is to remember that God is Father. You are good because God is good.

Getting to know God as Father, and that my worth, gifts and ability are there because of God's goodness, that's the important bit. So Jesus says, 'Don't be afraid. You see those little sparrows, even they are so precious to God our Father. You are of much more value than sparrows. His eye is on the sparrow and I know he's watching me lovingly. Every hair is counted because we are God's concern.

You are worth more than the hundreds of sparrows. Don't be afraid. *Mt 10:24-33*

Ordinary Time Week 15: Monday

A special prize was offered for a painting of a 'Peace Scene'. One artist sketched nature's quiet, with mountains, lake, sky and colours in contrast. The second artist presented a canvas of a raging, tumbling waterfall, foaming with white froth, and underneath the fall was a little bird sitting in her nest with her chicks. The bird and her chicks were living in a challenging noisy world of power and dangers. The bird and chicks won the prize for peace.

Peace-making is not about easy living and smiles. Peace-making hurts and humiliates the maker. It never gives up, is always looking for a way, gets involved. Parents are nature's peace-makers, keeping the balance, trying to understand the different ages, giving rope to grow but not enough to hang with, encouraging the 'internal spirit' of enthusiasm, generosity, creativity, even if the external practices of Mass-going and sacraments are put on hold for a time, by young people.

It is not peace I have come to bring but a sword. *Mt 10:34*

Ordinary Time Week 15: Tuesday

Maybe it's me, but I sense at times a terrible guilt that people carry, which is not of God. Saying to self, 'I never measure up. I'm not into religion myself. I don't have to go to Mass to be a Christian. It is only for the alright - not the all wrong.' Maybe it is due to a bad misunderstanding of catechism religion, maybe it is deeper. Maybe it is pre-occupation with sin that is soul destroying.

To blame God for all this guilt prompted Pope John XXIII to say that when some people give up on God, they are giving up on a false God anyway.

Where is the God of compassion, slow in anger, rich in mercy, that the heart longs for? One can sense the pain of Jesus trying to reach people's minds which want to remain ignorant of God as Father and self as human. It is heart therapy he chooses, not miracles.

Jesus began to reproach the towns in which his miracles had been worked. *Mt 11:20-24*

Ordinary Time Week 15: Wednesday

A lady was looking at a fuchsia yesterday. She said, 'Aren't they all little miracles? There are so many that they become common, almost un-noticed.' So Jesus says, 'Bless you, Father of heaven and earth.'

Another day full of life. Nature wanting to love us, and other people too. A baby smiles, a child laughs. We hear a funny story. All is given. We need eyes to see.

The mother said, 'I see every day as a Mass bread host. In every action I do, every thought I think, every fear, pain, joy, love. I'm just breaking pieces off that host that is Christ in whom I live, move and have my being.'

Everything has been entrusted to me by the Father. *Mt 11:25-27*

Ordinary Time Week 15: Thursday

Brendan is a good husband and family man. He works conscientiously. He finds extra time to help young people in the neighbourhood. I invited him to serve, giving Communion at Sunday Mass. He said, 'I'm not worthy for that. I leave that to blessed hands.'

I wonder does Christ want to be side-lined to holy hands and holy places? He talks with sinners and even eats with them. We are all sinners, but we are graced sinners. He wants to be with us in action, as companions, sharing bread of friendship. 'Come to me,' the over-burdened with guilt, fear, unworthiness. He calls our everyday struggles with ourselves and others his own. 'Take up my yoke,' he says. Our awkward harness of weakness he calls his own. 'I am with you.' We need to relearn the words of Jesus, not by rote, but by heart.

Come to me ... Shoulder my yoke. *Mt 11:28-30*

Ordinary Time Week 15: Friday

A parish sister in Liverpool defaced a public poster. The poster suggested that there were jobs for young people but that they were too lazy to take on work. Did she realise that what she was doing was illegal or breaking the law? She said that she never thought of that. It was the injustice that was being done to young people that kept annoying her.

Jesus was always trying to rid people of injustice and superstitious laws that crushed humanity and belittled their dignity, like the sick accused of being unclean or the disabled being ignored. The one who cares enough to help another is observing the Spirit of the Sabbath, even though he may not go to the Temple.

What I want is mercy. The Son of Man is Lord of the Sabbath.
Mt 12:5

Ordinary Time Week 15: Saturday

Alexander Torea went into hiding during Church persecution in Romania. He was tracked down and spent many years in prison. Pressure by western leaders helped his release, but he was strictly forbidden to practice as a priest. The people would ask him to come and bury their dead with a prayer. So he was arrested again after a funeral. He was asked to explain why he kept breaking the law and being a threat to the State. He said, 'If the people have courage enough to ask me to pray with them, I must have the courage to be with them.' He said, 'All you have to do is put me in prison again if you want to stop me.'

The people's faith and encouragement gave Alexander faith and courage. Even though Jesus was a wanted man, many followed him and I am sure gave him encouragement.

They began to plot against Jesus ... but many followed him.
Mt 12:14-21

Ordinary Time Week 16: Monday

A shopkeeper had a dream that Jesus would visit his shop next day. He was full of expectation. A woman arrived at the shop giving out about prices. She bought a bottle of milk. A travelling man arrived looking for a free loaf. Children arrived with no money but inquiring about prices. Another arrived looking for change. Closing time came and there was no sign of Jesus. The shopkeeper went to Mass and he heard the priest read the words of Jesus, 'I was hungry and you gave me to eat. I was a stranger and you took me in.' Suddenly he realised Jesus had come and does come, but we don't recognise him in such ordinary clothes.

The signs of God's presence are there, strange faces and strange places, awkward customers like Jonah, people that cross my path. The signs are all right but my vision is weak.

The only sign I will give is the sign of the prophet Jonah.

Mt 12:38-42

Ordinary Time Week 16: Tuesday

A young man of nineteen came to talk about religion. 'I'm interested in reading about religion,' he said, 'and reading the Bible. I'm trying to find my way.' I felt very good to be asked about God and living life. 'The words I like best in the Gospel,' he said, 'are where Jesus said, 'Here are my mother and brothers and sisters,' pointing to all the people.' I asked why. He said, 'It means everybody is equal, every one is the same to God. We are all God's favourites.' He liked the idea that we are forgiven by God Our Father all the time, through the people who live with us, work for us, tolerate us, smile at us. Every sunrise, every breath, is a sign of refreshment and forgiveness. Coming together with others from time to time to celebrate forgiveness he thought a good idea.

Who is my mother, who are my brothers? *Mt 12:46-50*

Ordinary Time Week 16: Wednesday

'We can worry too much about people's religious practices,' the lecturer said. People carry their own sense of God in their hearts. There is an inside religion and outside devotion. God was with the people as they journeyed. They hadn't churches. They got manna on the way. God was a daily presence.

A mother was explaining to me that formal prayer might not be too popular with the children, but to sprinkle the day with casual prayer was acceptable. But most important was her own attitudes to life and way of behaving in relation to people and property.

God is present with us sometimes in patches of rock, sometimes among thorns, sometimes in rich soil.

Some seeds fall on the edge. *Mt 13:1-9*

Ordinary Time Week 16: Thursday

The world we live in is God's shop window, with never-ending displays of clouds and colours, mountain reflections in lakes, animal and bird life that delights us. Nature mounts a new show every day, in season and out of season, and there is the world of people that cross our path everyday. All the happenings and events which some call luck or fate, others see as God's providence, a mystery never totally grasped, but which promises golden moments at the end of the rainbow.

Jesus constantly invites us to see and to hear. A sad partner said, 'He looks at me but he doesn't see me.' Seeing is of the heart. It is sensitivity. It is wanting to understand. So it is that we can hear but not listen - again the hearing is in the heart. How challenging to really listen, even to pick up the unspoken, the hint of pain one longs to express, not wanting solutions but a listening heart. Our seeing and listening hearts are blessed in baptism. May God's gifts come alive in us, bring joy to self, family, friends, neighbours and all we meet.

Happy are your eyes because they see, your ears because they hear. *Mt 13:10-17*

Ordinary Time Week 16: Friday

The Marriage Counsellor spoke about a young couple. She picks up the baby in the evening, returns home, prepares the evening meal, gives time to the baby, before settling down to bed. He returns home, switches on TV, sits down to read the papers. She serves the dinner and tidies up afterwards and begins to prepare for tomorrow, wash a blouse and his shirt, get ready his lunch or her lunch. He watches TV. Eventually they retire to bed, and he wonders why their marriage intimacy is not great.

The Counsellor says it is like hearing without understanding. She says that it takes so little to try to understand the feelings of another – a word of praise, a single rose, a birthday remembered. Maybe it is only a story from one side. Nagging, hurtful words and accusations wither the strings of love too. There is a time and a way to speak. There is a time and a way to be silent.

The man who hears and understands yields a harvest. *Mt 13:18-23*

Ordinary Time Week 16: Saturday

A little girl was riding her bicycle through the bright flowers in our garden. I said, 'Look, love, you are hurting the flowers. They want to live too.' She said, 'But it is not my bike, it is my brother's!'

There are weeds and wounds in our make-up. Even our best gifts and talents are soiled. But the poet says, 'We have to learn to dance on a moving carpet. The weeds don't go away in Jesus's story and we don't know why. Maybe our weakness and failings are our passports to heaven. The man with a new heart said, 'There would be no love in the world without suffering and pain.'

When you weed out the dead kernel, you might pull up the wheat with it. *Mt 13:24-30*

Ordinary Time Week 17: Monday

Matt said, 'We must have a Sports Day for the children this year.' The little ones racing is best of all. We had won various gold and silver medals in senior school ranks. Stardom is alright, but the little ones have their own charm. The kingdom of God is made up of the little ones and the stars, strong and weak, saints and sinners, all the same in God's eyes.

The little ones are all of us who give taste to life, in cooking and cleaning and greeting and celebrating, planning and hoping and wishing. The stars maybe find extra time to be more caring for the suffering of others.

I will expound things hidden since the foundation of the world. *Mt 13:31-35*

Ordinary Time Week 17: Tuesday

First Communion began the day I was conceived, when I began to belong to God, to my parents, family and thousands of people through life. I like the idea of Communion and Mass as celebrating that bond, that friendship with God and with all people in the human family. I don't 'make' Communion so much as find Communion. Communion is there to celebrate in the living of life.

I like the idea of Mass happening outside church more than in church, in the sharing of life and the giving of life in all kinds of ways, at home and among the crowds. Celebrating the breaking of bread takes in the anxiety, pains, disappointment and limitations of everyday life.

Leaving the crowds, Jesus went to the house. *Mt 13:36–43*

Ordinary Time Week 17: Wednesday

Do children play hide and seek now? God presents himself as a hide and seek God. He hides and he seeks and it is exciting.

The young courier delighted us with her words. We were on a magic train – the Clonmacnoise West Offaly Express – a mystery tour in a wonderland, the bog. She said, 'The bog is nature's refrigerator, a perfect preserver. A human body over a thousand years old, a butter churn three hundred years old.' We got souvenirs: moss that heals wounds, a sundew plant which feeds on catching insects - when refined it is a cure for Whooping Cough.

God is in the searching and in the finding. We're never mere spectators or on the sideline in God's team. We're active players, Jesus, Moses, me and you.

The kingdom of God is like a treasure hidden in a field. *Mt 13:44-46*

Ordinary Time Week 17: Thursday

We're a mixed bag in our make-up. The lady said that she liked the Catholic religion because it had a place for the sinner, the weak, the mixed-up. It was not too straight-laced or legalistic.

The Church accepts the mix-up that is me. I am good but never perfect. He talked with sinners and even ate with them. What a scandal that God loves first!

We are a haul of all kinds. *Mt 13:47-53*

Ordinary Time Week 17: Friday

The Dead Poets Society is a movie about a teacher. It was the way he taught his pupils that got him into trouble. For him, education was about appreciating oneself, one's gifts and talents, appreciating other people and life itself. The headmaster was keen on results. Rules had to be observed to ensure results. Conform or else. The film ends with the dullest one in class graduating in character and manliness. So the fight was worth it, even if the teacher lost his job.

In his home town, Jesus taught the people in such a way that they were astonished at his wisdom, yet rejected him. So when the youngsters reject the wisdom of parents for the time being, or the wisdom of Church, it won't be the first or the last time and it doesn't mean that parents or Church are always wrong. Life is full of surprises.

Where did he get this wisdom? ... and they would not accept. *Mt 13:54-58*

Ordinary Time Week 17: Saturday

Why did God let my partner have an affair? Why did God take that young mother? Why did my child have to be sick and handicapped? Why have I no job or friends? Why am I at all? Why am I as I am? Why do bad things happen to good people? Why did Jesus let his cousin be put in prison and have his head cut off for a dancing girl?

There are no answers. Maybe we think too much of God as a God of power, whereas he is more the God of restraint, the God who waits for us. Passion means waiting.

God's only power is love, and love does not use force. Love respects freedom, so love invites but does not compel. God does not promise to take away challenge, struggle, pain, even sin, but promises always to help us through our problems. He is present in the darkness. The novel *City Girl* tells the experiences of three girls in to-day's world and how, through friendship, they survive and become more beautiful.

They took the body and buried it and then went off to tell Jesus. *Mt 14:1-12*

Ordinary Time Week 18: Monday

Irene, a Russian girl, was imprisoned for writing poetry. She suffered greatly with cold and hunger. She explained how 'warmers' helped her to survive. In her harsh prison cell was a mug. With that mug, she was able to tap messages to another prisoner along the single pipe line that ran through the cell. That message, communication with another human, being kept her alive. She called it a 'warmer'. She said when a prisoner would share a piece of food that was stolen when one was weak with hunger, they called it a 'warmer' too.

Mass celebrates the warmers of word and food – a Christ presence. We are encouraged through Mass to be warmers in life to others, not freezers. We are warmed by praise, by touch, by helping hands, by sensitive listening.

Give them something to eat yourselves. *Mt 14:13-21*

Ordinary Time Week 18: Tuesday

Last summer I visited the Blasket island, Blasket Mór. We took a small boat from Dunquin harbour. I recall my feelings descending that winding cliff-rock stairs. The frail little boat, far below, bobs and bows in the water. It waits to take on the mighty ocean. We are a cargo of twelve people. There is a kind of uneasy conversation as we go on board. As we meet the first waves, I have a feeling of dependency. There are just light sheets of wood between me and the frightening depths of the sea. I can even touch the water with my hand. The island ahead draws in welcome and interest. The mainland home-base recedes reluctantly. Our moorings are cut now.

The feelings suggest that we are a people caught up in a wondrous mystery. Life has within it frailty and fear, wonder and awe, dependency, hope, adventure and joy.

Today the Lord seems to direct operations in a boat on the waters. He takes our frailty into his providence. He is with us through the rough crossings of life and death. We are drawn to a new island, full of wonder and mystery and generosity. It will be picnic time.

Lord, tell me to come to you across the water. *Mt 14:22-36*

Ordinary Time Week 18: Wednesday

An old Jewish man collapsed on the street. He was dying. A Catholic priest stopped. He bent low and asked the man if he believed in God the Father, God the Son and God the Holy Spirit. The old man opened his eyes and said, 'Why do you talk to me in riddles when I am a dying man?'

People in pain or worried and anxious, don't get involved in theological discussions or prayer methods. They cry from the heart for help.

Granny died yesterday. Her most loved possession was her deceased husband's rosary beads, broken, repaired and kept together with safety pins. Those beads recorded thousands of heart-prayers for help through years of uncertainty – a treasured Diary of Days waiting on God.

Woman you have great faith. *Mt 15:21-28*

Ordinary Time Week 18: Thursday

When Bad things happen to Good People is the name of a book written by a Jewish Rabbi. He suffered the loss of wife and child. Why this should happen? He does not know. There is no answer. But when suffering and tragedy come, he says that God is present, helping us through the pain and agony.

Jesus says, 'I must go through the journey of pain.' Peter says, 'That must never happen to you.' Happen it does, to all of us. When it does happen God, hidden in the darkness, comes in the carriage with you.

Peter started to remonstrate with Jesus. 'This must not happen to you.' *Mt 16:13-23*

Ordinary Time Week 18: Friday

A.A. people and Gambling Anonymous always impress me. I think it is the sheer truth of their programme, found through suffering. They live one day at a time. They depend on help from God. One man explained that his problem was that he had lost self-worth. 'It was getting this inner me right,' he said, 'that was necessary. No drugs, drink and money can supply that need, take its place, or make up for its loss.'

People who cannot accept that they are weak and vulnerable have a problem. We put up all kinds of excuses and explanations to avoid self. It is called rejection - rejecting the reality, the reality that is me, wounded but good, dependant but a child of God. Jesus says he is our human anchor.

Anyone who loses his life for my sake will find it. *Mt 16:24-28*

Ordinary Time Week 18: Saturday

They were happy together, just the two of them in their own little cottage. He found her dead by the fireside one evening. The shock made him sick in his mind and he burned the cottage one night, crying, 'There was two of everything. There will be one of nothing.' They brought him to the asylum and they called him the man who never had a visitor. He kept saying, 'There were two of everything. There will be one of nothing.'

The nothingness of loneliness, feeling unloved, excluded, rejected. This nothingness Jesus came to heal, to bring people together, to ease the journey of loneliness, to foster companionship, which means eating and drinking in friendship. Bless all who work in this ministry, for the heart is a lonely hunter.

Lord take pity on my son: he is a lunatic. *Mt 17:14-20*

Ordinary Time Week 19: Monday

The star footballer of yesterday is irritated that he cannot get a ticket for the game to-day. A complimentary ticket is a perk. Privilege is nice, but it is not the way life is.

Sometimes for one's peace and, as the Lord said, not to offend others, it is good to stand in the queues of life. There can be blessings in the waiting too. Someone gives you a laugh. Someone has always a better or sadder story.

The nurse said, 'The patients are fine and indeed grateful. It is often the healthy relatives that give us problems.' We are funny. How we forget all that is going for us, and think of things we haven't got.

'Give them the half Shekel tax.' One senses a carefree attitude in Jesus about things.

Give the shekel to them for you and for me. *Mt 17:22-27*

Ordinary Time Week 19: Tuesday

They told me that he was a stray dog. He came and never left.

There is beauty and mystery about stray people too. Maybe it is our nature to stray. But we should be reassured that we have a Father who cares lovingly. His eye is on the sparrow and I know he is watching me.

Jesus spoke of joy when strays unite at home. The graffiti artist wrote his name every night in a public place. Each day the authorities erased the name. It stopped after fifteen productions. Either the artist had made his name, and was now satisfied, or he got tired of straying and he came home.

He will leave the ninety-nine and go in search of the stray.
Mt 18:12-14

Ordinary Time Week 19: Wednesday

The Marriage Counsellor explained that people want more out of marriage now a days – that it is quite wrong to accuse people of being more selfish and permissive.

There is need for more equality, sharing together, decision-making together, especially when you're living with part-time work and being away from home. The happiness of the couple is the basic happiness and takes precedence over the child's happiness.

'Listing the faults of a partner, moralising, is a disaster,' he said, 'What we call selfish, looking for notice, is often a deep lack of affection, a cry to be understood.'

Marriage partners have a great need to be healed by each other. They also have the power to heal, because all humanity is graced.

Where two or three meet in my name, I shall be there with them.
Mt 18:15-20

Ordinary Time Week 19: Thursday

Mary did not come to the parish meeting. They said that she is giving up parish work because of something the priest said. I felt that Mary had misunderstood. Her little boy was excluded from playing around the church in a dangerous area. I waited for months wondering how to handle this situation. To say sorry for something I felt right to do, was not truth. To let silence and misunderstanding grow was not truth. So I went to Mary. I said, 'Look, I feel that you are hurt. I just want you to know that there was no hurt intended. I act that way, that is me. I am a human being with limitations but I felt I had to say a word for a little boy's own safety.' Mary said, 'I was only upset because you were upset.' There was tea and a chat and joy exchanged. I can still remember how light and happy my heart felt leaving that house.

I think that is why Jesus asks us to go first and talk because that will relieve the pain and anxiety in our own hearts. Then we can celebrate God's forgiveness.

Lord, how often must I forgive? *Mt 18:21*

Ordinary Time Week 19: Friday

I never met anyone who went into marriage with divorce in mind. Human nature being what it is, things go wrong. Life can become very difficult indeed, and with all that goes a yearning to be wanted, to feel special. The heart is a lonely hunter.

We sometimes smile, hearing of a third, fourth, fifth divorce or re-marriage. We grasp at straws to ease the thirst of loneliness. We say that the children suffer and that is true – a further pain to cope with.

The Church tries to be the compassionate mother but, in doing so, does not want to make life more painful. She believes in the capacity of people to grow in love. The Church still loves those who have to walk alone and wants new life for them. We are never excluded from God's blessing, but welcomed.

It was because you were so unteachable, Jesus said, that Moses allows you to divorce. *Mt 19:3-12*

Ordinary Time Week 19: Saturday

Mary Maloney's baby started a loud cry during the sermon. Soother, car-keys and change of position were of no avail. She was making for the door with the songster when the young priest called her attention, saying, 'No need to take your little child out of God's Church. The child isn't annoying me.' The mother replied, 'I know, father, but you're annoying him.'

Those of us educated to the quiet Mass find the renewed Mass of people-participation very challenging indeed - maybe irritating. There is no perfection but, as a man said, he never yet heard a priest preaching that it was good to kill, steal or be unjust. We are encouraged to forgive and give life, however faulty the presentation.

Mass is about looking at each other, touching lives, and caring in God's name with God's blessing.

People brought little children to Jesus. *Mt 19:13-15*

Ordinary Time Week 20: Monday

The little child is playing with broken glass, coloured tablets, plastic bags. The parent, instead of giving too many 'don'ts' and 'warnings', provides more attractive alternatives – paints, pictures, drawing, building, even eating ice-cream.

The Christian religion is not so much a 'don't' way of life as a 'do' way of life. Jesus invites us to be life-givers. There is, of course, killing, adultery, lies, stealing, squeezing the life out of people. We carry wounds but also great gifts and talents for giving life to others. Preoccupation with our wounds and weakness can stifle the great capacity we have to give life, with helping hands, encouraging words, and good humour.

What must I do to possess eternal life? *Mt 19:16-22*

Ordinary Time Week 20: Tuesday

I shouldn't say this, but they make me feel like a leper. I've been in hospital. I felt so hurt that none of my family called. I had to contact them. I am made to feel ashamed, because I am single, a kind of disgrace that has to be lived with. If I was married like the others, or even religious, that would be alright, but they seem to blame me for not being like others.

I am convinced that there can be a special value in single life. Some how if you're married, you have to 'have things' and be doing things. That is what catches the eye, even my mother's eye. If I haven't these things my family don't seem impressed. I have nothing but I feel that I own everything. I am conscious of the richness of Christ in my life. I suffer with him but there is a keen happiness. Having nothing is like fresh water I used to drink from a spring well at home. I pray knowing that God is there and that with him one can do anything. Single life is lonely only if I let it be.

This I tell in praise of Margaret, and the many Margarets that are hidden in God's Kingdom.

'Everyone who has left for the sake of my name – eternal life.'

Mt 19:23–30

Ordinary Time Week 20: Wednesday

Queueing for a Living is a radio programme. The interviewer goes around looking for queues of people at prisons, pawn shops, social service centres. Waiting in queues is a kind of poverty of spirit. It seems like doing nothing. Yet what impresses me so much is the character and dignity of people interviewed. There is a sadness, but joy too and peacefulness. 'I can manage with what I get. I've only myself to care for.' 'There are others worse off than me.' One senses the great variety and contrasts in God's kingdom. There's a place for the working and the money-making, and there is a place for those who stand and wait. Only God sifts out the mix. He cautions us about being envious of others. Who knows? Mother Teresa says the greatest disease in the world is not lack of money, but lack of love.

Why be envious because I am generous. *Mt 20:1-16*

Ordinary Time Week 20: Thursday

They forgot to invite me to the Christmas party. I decided to bury my pride and gate-crash the occasion. The welcome was good and it was one of the happiest nights of my life. I went home early. On the road I noticed a young man lying motionless in the dark. I woke him up and brought him home. My passing was a life-saver for him and a night to remember for me.

God is always inviting us. We have to make an effort to respond. God makes the sun rise, the rain fall, everyday. He renews the face of the earth constantly and abundantly. We see, feel, touch, hear his invitations in the people and places of everyday life.

They gathered everyone they could find, bad and good alike, to the wedding. *Mt 22:1-14*

Ordinary Time Week 20: Friday

Mary was eleven when her mother died. Now she had no life of her own. She was expected to housekeep for her father and two brothers. Her only satisfaction was to eat. She did eat excessively. She lost her self-confidence. Her friend convinced her to join a Health Club, to take exercise and to regulate her eating habits. That friendship gave Mary the strength to like herself.

Loving oneself in a wholesome way is a challenge and something we should pray about. We are asked to love neighbour as self, but we tend to forget the 'self' part. We find it difficult to be gentle with self. I am a good, specially gifted and talented person, but also wounded and soiled. We can be so preoccupied with our limitations, weakness and failures, that we become paralysed in our life-giving gifts. To say a word of praise, to say thanks, to admire a baby, to enjoy a sunset, or just to listen, laugh and chat, is to affirm life.

You must love your neighbour as yourself. *Mt 22:34-40*

Ordinary Time Week 20: Saturday

I listen to a young man on radio who interviews people who stand in queues, waiting. What impresses me is his compassion. Somehow he is able to tap the dignity of the person, with timely hesitation and comforting sighs. Truth is beautiful even when it is wrapped in pain and sadness.

I think the ultimate test of religion is compassion. The good Lord challenges the people of his day: 'You make heavy burdens for people and don't lift a finger to help.' We have to begin lifting fingers to help before we tell others what to do by words, action or laws. Etty Hillesun, who died in Auchwitz, said, 'Don't ask what people do. Ask what do they suffer.'

They tie up heavy burdens but will not lift a finger to move them. *Mt 23:1-12*

Ordinary Time Week 21: Monday

The missioners said, 'We don't bring God into situations or peoples. God is already there before us. Our work is finding the God that is there in the lives of people and then celebrating.'

I suppose that is what sacraments do. We celebrate the presence of God in earthly happenings – welcomes, lovings, sharings, forgivings – touching sadness and joy in life. We use water and bread and wine and oil and words. We listen, we touch, we give, we stand and wait.

'The world is charged with the grandeur of God.' Holy places help us to see that all is holy. Holy people help us to see that all humans are holy. All happenings and events are enriched with Christ's presence. We must not shut up the kingdom of Heaven that hides in paint, pottery and pans.

Shutting the kingdom of God in men's faces. *Mt 23:13-22*

Ordinary Time Week 21: Tuesday

Barney is retired now, but he goes to Lough Derg every year. It is a tough pilgrimage, even for a youngster. 'Why do you go?' I asked Barney. He said, 'I am a bit of a cowboy. But I suppose the real reason is thanksgiving. I've a young lad abroad. He is a bit mixed up, trying to get to grips with himself. I ask the Lord to reach out to him and help him to make good decisions. Now he is getting through pretty good.'

Barney is a social man, but he is a spirit person too. The inside of us is precious; if it is ignored there is a loss. People who know God tell us to search for him inside ourselves too. They say what is important is giving time to God, not technique or method.

Clean the inside of the cup or dish. *Mt 23:23-26*

Ordinary Time Week 21: Wednesday

I suppose we all imagine meeting God sometime. Some people who know God very well say that God will be making excuses for us, rather than we making excuses to him. Rather than God searching for faults, he will be showing us the goodness and good intentions we had and had forgotten.

A beautiful girl I know was tragically killed today. She never wanted the marriage. She agreed more out of fear and to placate the insistence of her suitor. Then she was lonely, longed for love, longed for company and the joy of meeting other young people, really because she loved life. It was an innocence, a cry from the heart, rather than any crime of unfaithfulness.

Psalm 138:

O Lord you know me. You know my longing, you know me inside and out, my feelings and thoughts. Even when I am plunged in the depth of despair, you are there to meet me. Even in the darkest of nights, you are there. You were present at my conception. You will surely be present at my re-birth.

Ordinary Time Week 21: Thursday

There is always more to be seen. We never stop growing. Christine died in her eighties. She kept her mind alert. She taught her little grandchild from the earliest years. She gave her an interest in seeds and flowers, plants and trees. She read the papers when she was able. She had her special radio and TV programmes and a real interest in horse-racing. They said she picked all the winners, but never backed them. When the priest called, she had to be ready in person and in place. She insisted on a cup of tea, or a going away gift. Christine was an awake person.

Happy the servant the master finds at his employment. *Mt 24:42-51*

Ordinary Time Week 21: Friday

All life is about waiting: waiting to grow, waiting to get better, waiting for the post, waiting for the bus. I sometimes take our family kids out on a treat. I used to get annoyed waiting. They were invariably late and there were always reasons.

I decided that it was better to light a candle than to curse the darkness. I decided to go prepared and make waiting positive, maybe even enjoyable. I bring a book, a magazine, or a diary I want to rewrite. I thank God for the idea. There are still new reasons for being late after thirty-five years – a marvel in itself.

The foolish did take lamps but with no oil. *Mt 25:1-13*

Ordinary Time Week 21: Saturday

She said that her passion in life was to become more sure of herself, to waken up to her own power and to use the talent that is hers. We are gifted and wounded, but we can over-emphasise the wounds.

In the book, *City Girl*, Maggie finds her husband unfaithful. She decides to take up writing. Eventually she writes a bestselling novel. This gives her strength to heal marriage wounds and brings her into contact with like-minded people. It awakens her husband to sorrow, appreciation and responsibility.

The secret, the lady said, is that we have to make choices, get our own act together first. Take risks. Burying the talent is no answer. Life is now. Live the present.

I was afraid. I hid your talent. *Mt 25:14-3*

Ordinary Time Week 22: Monday

Annette is a wife, a mother and a great character. She always challenges with the same question: 'Do you believe in life after death?' She is never convinced with my, 'I do, but we don't know much about after life.' It is life now that Jesus kept stressing. He encouraged us to be caring. He would tell us, 'Believe in life before death,' so he launches his mission programme with, 'I have come to bring good news to the poor now, to give new sight now.' Good words, but not accepted.

I think the saints of today are all around us in parents like Annette and people who live ordinary lives, forever thinking and caring and encouraging. There are endless ways of trying to make life good at home, in the neighbourhood and in the world community.

He has sent me to bring good news to the poor. *Lk 4:16-30*

Ordinary Time Week 22: Tuesday

Sheila was obsessed with having a baby. Every meeting, every conversation was the same topic. She was willing to beg, borrow, or steal to achieve her desire. She would suggest travelling to the most remote parts of the world. Then, for six months there was a silence. When we met, I experienced surprise. She explained that she came to realise that baby-longing had become an obsession, that she had become a bore. She decided to cut herself off from talking about this and to pray to God for help. 'I asked him not to take away my longing and love for children, but to break this chain that was strangling my life. God did help me,' she said. 'I have now a job that I like. I am able to be happy for others with their children. I've a new life.'

Jesus said, 'Be quiet,' and it went out without hurting him at all. *Lk 4:31-37*

Ordinary Time Week 22: Wednesday

A little boy said, 'When I wake it is my birthday.' God gives a new day when we wake. It is like a circle or a large firm pancake. Every action we do is like breaking a piece from the bread circle. God is in the circle this day and every part of it.

In the Jesus story to-day there are a lot of interesting slices of how to grow as human beings. He left the synagogue and moved on. It was one job at a time. He went to Simon's mother-in-law to ease her sickness and he laid his hands on her. We are challenged to touch each one we meet everyday for the better. We begin with those at home.

He left again, went to a lonely place. Some call it the mysterious inside space that is our root and God's presence. In these moments alone, he is prompted for the next slice of action – leaving again.

When daylight came they left the house. *Lk 4:38-44*

Ordinary Time Week 22: Thursday

I like the story of the University student. He was a very popular young man. It was his birthday and he went down to 'the local' expecting to celebrate with his pals. Nobody turned up. Half an hour before closing time, two friends casually arrived and, on the way home, a girl suggested having a coffee in the flat. When they arrived at the flat all seemed quiet, but when the door opened he was greeted with a chorus of song from all his friends, 'For he's a jolly good fellow!' plus lights and decorations, food and drink. There were hugs, greetings, presents, cards and a birthday cake. He felt embarrassed and a little ashamed of his 'bad thoughts' about them, when he was now experiencing lavish generosity.

It was the mood of Peter – a generous enthusiastic man, but when he met utter generosity and extravagant goodness he was embarrassed with joy. I guess heaven is that extravagant God.

Leave me Lord, I am a sinful man. *Lk 5:1-11*

Ordinary Time Week 22: Friday

I danced in the morning when the world was begun.
I danced on the moon, on the stars, on the sun.
I came down from Heaven and I danced on the earth.
At Bethlehem I had my birth.
'Dance, Dance wherever you many be,
I am the Lord of the dance,' said he,
'and I'll lead you all wherever you may be.
and I'll lead you all in the dance,' said he.

Who are we singing about? What are we singing about? Jesus says it is dancing time. The rainy day will come. Now is joy time.

Paul gives the most powerful words ever written: 'Christ is the first born of all creation.' In him we're created, all things, heaven and earth – pottery, painting, scribbling, sights and sounds, tastes and smells, purring cats, friendly dogs. Yes, kisses, cuddles, fortunes, jokes, pain, brokenness. No wonder the monks rise to sing.

Come before the Lord to sing with joy. Serve the Lord with gladness. *Ps 99*

Ordinary Time Week 22: Saturday

Johnny goes to Mass, but is bored. He never gets involved in the celebration. The Mass, in the sense of a caring for others in day to day living, says nothing to him.

Kathleen does not go to Mass, but she is very taken by small groups of similar interest. There is friendliness and participation - a feeling of God present and a concern for others. Jackie is not into Mass or prayer groups but is a people person. A fast for the poor, a walk for the handicapped, a man on call for anything in the community, a justice person, a green-peacer, a God-in-the-heart kind.

All three have appeal and good points. It is a foolish person that would judge another's religion or tell the full story of faith. Only God is master of the sabbath in our lives.

The Son of man is master of the sabbath. *Lk 6:1-5*

Ordinary Time Week 23: Monday

Whenever George raised a drink to his lips, he would say, 'May the giving hand never wither. Thanks for the treat.' Withering starts in the heart and can result in tight fist, a tight purse, and tight lips (no words of praise).

I have a feeling that in to-day's story Jesus is trying to resuscitate the man's heart with a kind of shock therapy. 'Stand up¡ Come out! Stretch out your hand!' It is rather like my mother telling me to stand straight, present yourself properly. Jesus is saying that we have a lot going for us, no looking back at ourselves or others begrudgingly. Jesus can reach the child in us to see and use the talent we're given. Be a stretching hand - a helping hand.

Stand up! Come out! Stretch out your hand! *Lk 6:6-11*

Ordinary Time Week 23: Tuesday

All work and no play makes Jack a dull boy and Mary a dull girl. Do we believe this? God our Father invites us to take time to play. He calls it prayer. A famous saint and scholar calls prayer 'recreation time'. It is for our advantage, our fulfilment, but done for God's sake It is not so much twisting God's arm to do our way as letting him teach us his way. It is called waiting – some time given to waiting for God – no words needed. It is not thinking about God. It is more like waiting to let God talk.

Everybody prays because the spirit of God is with everyone. How often we have met people who had not the external practices of religion but had deep faith in the way they saw people and life. I think of Etty Hillesun who died in Auchwitz. God is deep in the recesses of her beautiful humanity. She was able to be with others and for others. She was able to keep in touch because of awareness of God's presence.

Jesus went out into the hills to pray. *Lk 6:12-19*

Ordinary Time Week 23: Wednesday

We're trying to get a little group of people together to visit homes, especially the homes of newcomers. We made up a name: 'C.A.S.H.' 'Calling and Saying Hello.'

When the word 'poor' is mentioned we tend to think of poverty, stricken and far away, rather than of ourselves or our neighbours. There are a thousand different faces of the 'poor'. A survey recently found that the richest children in school were the most deprived emotionally. There is the poverty of being afraid, not knowing anybody, of shyness.

Jesus counted us all in when he said, 'Blessed are the poor.' It is a present condition, as near as myself or the person I meet.

How happy are you who are poor. *Lk 6:20-26*

Ordinary Time Week 23: Thursday

Brian Keenan, the hostage, was able to forgive his enemies and torturers. He said 'They didn't know what they were doing.' This helped his sanity.

I sensed that John was avoiding me. There had been an incident involving his child playing dangerously in the Church. I had to take action. It was misunderstood. I eventually got the courage to go to the child's home and put my cards on the table.

I said I could sense some hurt. There was no hurt intended. The parents were greatly pleased and relieved. They explained that they felt bad because of the hurt that was caused to me. I can still remember the feeling of well-being leaving that home – a feeling of being released.

God our Father helps us to release ourselves from unnecessary burdens and hang-ups.

Treat others as you would like them to treat you. *Lk 6:27-38*

Ordinary Time Week 23: Friday

Has God a sense of humour? He must have or else there would not be so much humour in the world. The Jesus story today has humour in it.

He asks why do we observe little splinters in the eyes of others and miss a plank of splinters in our own. We can't help noticing splinters in others that irritate us, but the Lord is saying that we are blind to our own. How can we get balance? 'There, but for the grace of God, go I.' Notice that when I point a finger of accusation at another, there are three fingers pointing back at myself.

Take the plank out of your own eye first. *Lk 6:39-42*

Ordinary Time Week 23: Saturday

The student said that he was selling the potted plants for depressed people. He explained that we want more people to be aware that depression is a normal sickness, and that there is help available. A chat-show talked over the subject. One said that over-stress on 'I'm worthless, of no use, of no value,' was one way to depression. Another said that images of oneself are important, that one has a spiritual paralysis, a drowning feeling during depression.

I thought that if our image of God was good it might help self image. Jesus tries so much to give us that self worth. 'You are my friends.' There is an inside person that is beautiful. There are resources there. I like the Church's prayer: 'Thank you God for loving me. I'm sorry for not loving others and for not loving you.' 'Thank you' comes first.

A good man brings good out of the treasure of good things in his heart. *Lk 6:43-49*

Ordinary Time Week 24: Monday

Cancer had weakened all Margaret's bones. She could not even turn or move her hands a few inches. Yet she thought only of others, organising little presents for her husband, for the doctors, for her visitors. She longed to go home but that wasn't possible. She was grateful that 'home' came to her in the form of family visits and friends.

As it happened, she had no faith in God or life hereafter. Her faith was in love and loving people.

Jesus was constantly teaching that God Our Father touches all people's hearts. We are all his favourites.

Lord I am not worthy ... Say the word and I shall be healed. *Lk 7:1-10*

Ordinary Time Week 24: Tuesday

Jean Vanier is to-day's saint of the mentally handicapped. He says that people sometimes ask him, 'How can you do this kind of work? You must be very holy to be close to dying people, to useless people, to smelly people.' Strangely, he says it is not like that. To be close to people with handicaps, to enjoy their company, you have to be in contact with your own handicaps, learning to live with them and, I dare say, enjoy them. Can we be compassionate to ourselves?

Jesus is humanity in touch with himself in to-day's story. Touching that stretcher with the dead body was illegal and would have made him unclean, unworthy of the Temple. Because Jesus was so much in touch with his own humanity, so sensitive to human needs, he broke through the barriers that make people feel worthless, diseased, separated. He affirms life, not only after death but now.

He went up and put his hand on the bier. *Lk 7:11-17*

Ordinary Time Week 24: Wednesday

Jesus was called a drunkard and a glutton because he ate and drank with the ordinary people. One spiritual writer said that Mary Magdalen's perfume and kiss gave Jesus the strength he needed that night to go through with his ordeal. Love is never lost, least of all when poured over dead losses.

Awaiting a cancer operation, Mary said, 'It is good of you to come in. You know I like you.' 'I like you too.' I could sense the consoling presence of him loving us. The friend of drunkard and glutton.

You say, 'Look, a glutton and a drunkard.' *Lk 7:31-35*

Ordinary Time Week 24: Thursday

We've been trying for months to launch C.A.S.H., 'Calling and Saying Hello,' a small group who would visit homes in the parish with a word of welcome and information about goings on. I asked Fourth Class children how they would re-act to the callers. 'Come in. Sit down. Have a cup of tea. Have a nice day. Thanks for calling,' were some of the responses. I asked, 'If Mom was very busy getting the tea, what would you say?' A little girl answered spontaneously, 'I'd ask them to join us for tea.'

Mary Magdalen gave the attention of hospitality to Jesus. Love was poured out and somehow that is so marvellous that all other failings are washed clean in God's eyes.

A woman with a bad name is touching him. *Lk 7:36-50*

Ordinary Time Week 24: Friday

If a person wanted to join the Church and asked for one book to read what book would you give? I think I'd give St Luke's gospel. He shows us the humanness of Christ. I think we need that most. He touches the heart with his human stories that reveal the great compassion of God for his weak, wounded, favourite children. Luke had a sensitive eye and a thoughtful heart for women. He brings beautiful women characters into the life of Jesus. That would be a shocker in his day. He went to villages and towns with good news and with twelve companions and certain women who had been cured – another shocker!

With him certain women, Magdalene, Joanna, Susanna and several others. *Lk 8:1-3*

Ordinary Time Week 24: Saturday

A retired teacher was advising a young teacher. He said, The day you feel that all the pupils are dumb and dull, the Principal a bore, the inspector an anachronism, and the parish priest a tyrant, take a change or a holiday.' He said teaching is like unlocking a burglar alarm – what code do you tap in to release the treasure? You can never predict the treasure: the fellow you thought might be pope or president you find behind bars, and the one you thought had little to offer turns out to be a great, caring human being.

The seeds of God's blessings are thrown at us in abundance. How the blessings are received is a great mystery. Hearts go astray. We get into a mess. Somehow God's love is infinitely coaxing. What we lose on the swings may be gained on the roundabouts of life.

A sower went out to sow his seeds. *Lk 8:4-15*

Ordinary Time Week 25: Monday

Everybody has a talent to share. I think of two problems about talents. We find it difficult to believe that we have a talent until others love us into believing in ourselves. Then when we believe in our talent, we can become overbearing and arrogant, forgetting the giver of talents.

Let your light be seen by others to the praise of God Our Father. We have plenty of singing talents but it is hard to get it going on Sundays. The last leader gave up. She said, 'They just won't sing.'

Maybe we've been pushing for perfection. If one can muster a note at all, give the 'kick start', and then fade out quickly, it is surprising the powerful participation that emerges. They only want a match to be struck, not a blaze of flame!

So that people may see the light. *Lk 8:16–18*

Ordinary Time Week 25: Tuesday

I like celebrating grandparents at Baptism time. One day a grandparent having held and blessed the baby said to me 'that was great.' She thought that grandparents were becoming redundant in the Church. Rembrand paints 'The Divine' in the faces of grandparents and elderly. He sees wisdomed achievement in furrowed features. We will be redundant the day we fail to notice these mighty blessings - sitting on granda's knee, going for walks, celebrating all the little occasions of growing up, being told that we are good and precious not because we win, not because we are successes but because I am just 'me'. The wisdom that praises rather than preaches or instructs is the grandparent blessing. The wisdom that listens to the young at heart, rather than always telling is 'grace' in action. God knows there are the limitations of poor health that makes us grumpy and cranky, but if we have tried to 'Mol an óige,' they in turn will find excuses for us and time for affection for blessings given.

'My mother and brothers are those who hear the Word of God.'

Lk 8:19–21

Ordinary Time Week 25: Wednesday

What is this good news that Jesus brought us? The newspaper man said that daily life for people is getting up in the morning, working, walking the floor with young children at night, having to watch what the kids like on TV, paying good money for books and clothes and family holidays instead of a few extras for themselves or the odd visit to an expensive restaurant.

All this is unselfish, and everytime people do this they get closer to God and to building his kingdom, even though it is ordinary and humdrum. That is the good news.

They set out ... proclaiming the good news. *Lk 9:1-6*

Ordinary Time Week 25: Thursday

She is a person I admire. She paints, reads, entertains, keeps in touch with what's going on, in touch with God especially in moments of silence. She plans to help in the local area, teaching children. It is not enough to be anxious to see Jesus. We must make an effort to 'do'.

I like the story of the Jewish exiles. They returned from slavery full of enthusiasm to rebuild their broken Temple. In forgetting the Temple they forgot the neighbour too. So the neighbour suffered and the country was worse off. 'The wage-earner gets his wages only to put them in a purse riddled with holes.'

Love of God calls for practical action, not vague wishes.

He was anxious to see Jesus. *Lk 9:7-9*

Ordinary Time Week 25: Friday

'They did not understand, and were afraid to ask questions.' Parents say that about children sometimes. Jesus said it about his companions. The greatest teacher the world has ever heard said that they did not understand because he was talking about pain, failure, and death. We don't want to hear about things like that. But Jesus is a realist. Pain, disappointment, sadness, do come our way. They are there in the living of marriage, in separation, in single life, in rich and poor and innocent. Jesus says, 'I am a co-sufferer with you. Trust me.'

The Son of Man is to suffer grievously. *Lk 9:18-22*

Ordinary Time Week 25: Saturday

Hughie is coming back to-day. He gave his life to the building work in England. Everyone was full of admiration for all he did as a husband, a father and a community man. 'The best foreman on the job,' they said. Men who never saw the inside of a church came to pay their respects. He died at his work in the trenches. He wished to be taken home to his country in the shade of the Slieve Bloom mountains. He loved a pint and chat-time with the lads. He backed a horse. He went through his fair share of suffering. He was refined and more human through it all.

Like the bewildered companions of Jesus, we don't understand. It is hidden from us now. But the story of Jesus says to us, 'Pick up the broken pieces. Stick with the job.'

Everyone was full of admiration for all he did. *Lk 9:43-45*

Ordinary Time Week 26: Monday

God is big-minded. When we see all the shenanigans that pre-occupy humans in private and public life, we have to marvel at the Mastermind. We are great and mischievous. We get rope enough to hang ourselves or make circles of love.

God has a million channels of truth. Sometimes people and even Churches are tempted to limit God to one channel. But God roams free and is full of surprises.

If good is done, Jesus says it doesn't matter who does it. Followers of Christ are called to be big-minded, like God Our Father.

Because he is not with us, we tried to stop him. *Lk 9:46-50*

Ordinary Time Week 26: Tuesday

They are one of the most loving families I know. The sixteen-year-old had an unexpected baby last year. The parents welcomed the baby into the family and supported their daughter in every way. They got her back to school. They sang the praise of Sister in Charge who was so understanding. But she broke from school, and runs away for days, sometimes a week, roaming the streets. The parents go into the city centre looking for her at night. The father explained that last week when she returned home, his heart filled with rage and love. She brought two stray eighteen year olds with her. He decided to bring her breakfast in bed the following morning.

Jesus resolutely took the road to Jerusalem. *Lk 9:51-56*

Ordinary Time Week 26: Wednesday

Eamon said, 'I'll tell you the difference between those two footballers. If you were in a spot of trouble and met Colin, he would be very pleasant and say, 'I'll help you tomorrow.' But if you met Michael, he'd go with you to-day to ease the trouble.'

Christ seems to say, 'Give it your best shot now. Eye on the ball, and don't look back too much.'. Down to business now. The present challenges.

No one who looks back is fit for the kingdom of God. *Lk 9:57-62*

Ordinary Time Week 26: Thursday

The Family Counsellor said, 'Remember that 'No' is a loving word too.' Young people need boundaries. They need the consistency of certain home rules. The young depend on us for guidance, even though it may not be appreciated at the time.

The loving 'No's' are not a curtailment of true freedom. They are a means of helping us to enjoy freedom in a human and wholesome way.

God's ten ways of truth are loving and life-giving 'No's'. The Lord reminds us that it is not always the 'Yes man' who delivers truth. He says, 'The kingdom of God is very near, in welcomes in healings and in rejections. Often the one who first says 'No' turns out to be a loyal and trusted friend. Such is the kingdom of God.'

And they do not make you welcome ... be sure the kingdom of God is near. *Lk 10:1-12*

Ordinary Time Week 26: Friday

When Samuel Morse invented the 'Morse Code' he thanked God for this wonder. When Neil Armstrong landed on the moon, he thanked man for this wondrous achievement. It is said that if we focus too much on the man-made and forget the maker of men, life becomes terribly boring. A mountain, a lake, the sea never fail to satisfy, but we get used quickly to the best of man-made things – ask the hostess on the Jumbo, the pilot on the Concorde, ask the millionaire who can travel the world and buy the most exclusive hotels or beaches. Even with colour TV we eventually get bored. If we can manage to listen to God, the man-made blessings become more refreshing.

A little boy was afraid to use his football lest it would get lost. Then his father told him, 'If it gets lost, I've got a better football waiting for you.' It took away his fear. He used a blessing wisely. Awareness of Our Father refreshes.

Anyone who listens to you, listens to me. Lk 10:13-16

Ordinary Time Week 26: Saturday

A famous spiritual writer says that faith is a 'way of seeing' rather than a set of beliefs. That God exists, like the North Pole, is not the question. The question is, 'Is God important to my living?'

Two people go into a hospital. One sees a human mess of sadness, pain and death. Another sees courage in people, loving care from hospital staff, support of friends and relations. It is the way one sees that is important.

'Happy the eyes that see what you see.' Those who know say that seeing comes from a presence of God.

Happy the eyes that see what you see. *Lk 10:17-24*

Ordinary Time Week 27: Monday

Maura went to the priest after his sermon. She complimented him on his scripture presentation, but added that she did not agree with his last sentence which was, 'If you don't follow this way God will disown you.'

The Good Samaritan God does not disown. He takes all kinds of risks in caring for the human person. He really puts himself out and comes back again.

I love the story of Jonah. The word 'jonah' means 'peace', but Jonah's idea of peace was 'sleeping', not putting yourself out for anyone or offering a helping hand. God had to teach him, that peace-making is a struggle, putting up with pain, settling rows, encouraging, praising.

The one who took pity ... Go and do the same.   *Lk 10:25-37*

Ordinary Time Week 27: Tuesday

The parish priest called to the house. The woman of the house asked, 'Would you like tea?' 'No.' 'Would you like coffee?' 'No.' 'Would you like a drink?' 'No. I want chat.'

I suppose that is a meaning of food and drink. It is a warm-up for chat. Yet too much chat is like a dripping tap – irritating when you notice it. A meal together is great. If the wash up and the tidy up starts too early after the meal, the chat suffers. It is a real art to balance serving and chatting. Who's to say which is more important? The Lord stresses the listening side of chatting or serving. Is that why we have two ears and one mouth - to listen twice as often as we talk?

Mary sat down at the Lord's feet and listened. *Lk 10:38-42*

Ordinary Time Week 27: Wednesday

Jesus gives the impression of being warmed, welcomed, strengthened when he goes away to pray. Is he saying that prayer is a renewal time, a refreshing time, when it is properly understood?

The people who know say the best prayer is to give time, waiting rather than using words. Wanting God to tell us what he is like, rather than telling him what he should do. That's why Jesus's sample prayer focuses on God Our Father first. The God present in our hearts flows out to human concern and care for the world.

Jesus was in a certain place praying. *Lk 11:1-4*

Ordinary Time Week 27: Thursday

I think if I was asked to advise young people preparing to be priests I would say, 'You are going to spend your lifetime asking.' We ask Baptism Friends to welcome new arrivals. We ask Confirmation Friends to host the youth. We ask for Communion Friends to celebrate with other families. We ask visiting Friends to bring welcome and information. We ask for readers/singers. We ask for leaders for our young people. We ask adults to help with stray little ones at Mass. We ask constantly for money to help others. Asking is good. Those who respond to asking 'blossom'.

Ask, Search, Knock. *Lk 11:5-13*

Ordinary Time Week 27: Friday

There is a saying that idle hands make work for devilment. I suppose that means that human beings are of special worth, treasured spirits that cannot be satisfied with junk ideas or the mere vacancy of non-living. Our spirit needs to be encouraged to flame and to be warmed into loving growth. I see this happening everyday. The little ones learn to paint and draw and go on nature walks to observe and admire. They investigate the secrets of science and display their findings for our attention.

I notice parents encouraging their children to say 'Thanks' and 'Sorry'. I see mistakes and failings overlooked and healed with loving forgiveness. People are encouraged to share, to make God's world a better place and to be sensitive to the home environment. To be swept and tidy is not enough for human hearts. We need the generosity of life-givers.

Swept and tidy ... the man ends up worse. *Lk 11:15-26*

Ordinary Time Week 27: Saturday

How can we pick up the sound of God's word in ordinary daily experiences? – the coming and goings, crossings and meetings, celebrations, and sadness? God does not wish to be side-lined to Sunday, holy things and holy places. He is the God of pots and pans, pains and problems, the God that walks with us. Mary was a pot-and-pan person who could celebrate joy, but also stand waiting loyally in time of pain. We ask her to teach us her secret. 'Holy Mary, pray for us sinners, now and at the hour of our death.'

Happy are those who hear the word of God.   *Lk 11:27-28*

Ordinary Time Week 27: Monday

The girls were mildly mentally handicapped. Sister organised a bus-outing and an overnight stay for them. There was a lot of preparation involved, a lot of caring and being present. Her assistant had a thing about getting morning Mass in. While Sister was getting her family ready and dressed for the holiday breakfast, her partner kept pestering her about the times of Mass for the morning. They could get the Franciscans at 11a.m. They could ... I don't know how the story ended. I just heard about the frustration endured.

It reminded me of how we read signs of God's presence. Is giving time, joy, patience not a real sign of God's presence? Is Mass the only sign of God's presence? Or is it a sign that helps us to appreciate and read the signs of his presence at our elbow – our own presence to people anywhere, anytime, any place. The Jonah story teaches us that God is present in the unlikely, the so-called failures, even in ourselves with all our funny ways.

The only sign I give is the sign of Jonah. *Lk 11:29-32*

Ordinary Time Week 28: Tuesday

There was a beautiful piece of stone art on exhibition. The shape, colour and outside features were a delight to eye and mind. The artist explained that it was the space inside the vessel that was really special. The outside design was made for the inside hollow.

'It is not emptiness, but rather mystery,' the artist was saying. We humans are vessels, made to contain a greatness we do not see, and we're waiting to be filled with this mystery. Some call this 'soul'. Prayer artists know best about this secret of God that is us. Jesus very often talks about this mystery. Gaining the whole world is nothing in comparison with this mystery of soul. It is not a vacant area but rather what makes us see and be, and pray, and love. Did not he who made the inside make the outside too? *Lk 11:37-41*

Ordinary Time Week 28: Wednesday

Etty Hillesum was a single girl. She volunteered to go with her people to the notorious concentration camp and she died in Auchwitz. The Diary of her life experiences makes wholesome reading. She touches all the human emotions.

She says, 'Don't ask people what they do. Ask them what they suffer.'

What do parents suffer, and a single parent in particular in bringing a child into the world? What does a couple suffer through courtship, working and saving and planning? What the separated and divorced suffer is often like death!

Life does not need extra rules, obligations, burdens. Who wants a lecture or a sermon? How we blossom and bloom with a word of praise and an assurance, 'You're alright'! We do like to be asked what suffering we've been through.

'Alas – because you load burdens' *Lk 11:42-46*

Ordinary Time Week 28: Thursday

It is said that it was Jesus's way of thinking, his challenging ideas, that got him into trouble. It is good when we are challenged about our attitudes to the hungry of the world, about vast money sums spent on arms. It is good when we are challenged about the travellers in our midst, our care for children, our concern for the weak and handicapped. It is good when we are challenged about what we give to community, to parish, to neighbour. It is good to be challenged about time spent on ourselves, and time given to others in any shape or form. Do we use wisely the blessings of life for our own good and the good of others? Jesus challenges the wisdom of greed, for our own good and for our sanity - so that we may have life.

The wisdom of God said, 'I will send them a prophet.' *Lk 11:47-54*

Ordinary Time Week 28: Friday

I had to preside over the interviews of eight teachers. Being Chairman is a bit like washing up at meal time. Instead of cursing my lot, I said I'd try to learn something, ask a question. But, my mind wandered off in boredom!

Do children wonder at things nowadays? is wonder being lost through saturation? The question was prompted by 300 crows. They all took off at the same time in a field nearby. They dived, circled, sped left and right. They did the most fantastic movements. They never crashed - not even one.

Jesus is always trying to alert us, make us alive to the wonder of our own being. 'You are so precious. You are my idea – warts and all. I know every hair, not one is forgotten.' Jesus says be on guard against seeing only rubbish in life. Everything will be made clear. 'To you, my friends, I say, don't be afraid, even of death. Look at those sparrows. Not even one is forgotten by the Father.'

Every hair on your head is counted – no need to be afraid. *Lk 12:1-7*

Ordinary Time Week 28: Saturday

Johnny said to me, 'I'll be home soon, with the help of God. I always say "with the help of God." I'd often be at home,' he said, 'wondering would I build a bit of a wall, or paint the house, and a neighbour would say, "That is a job you could do." A word like that can give you a little rev up, a reminder, an encouragement. I suppose that's the Holy Spirit. That's why I say, "with the help of God."'

Christ makes his presence felt through his Spirit in all kinds of people and all kinds of places. We are carried along on the Spirit's constant prayer of intercession. The Holy Spirit inside and outside.

The Holy Spirit will teach you. *Lk 12:8-12*

Ordinary Time Week 29: Monday

Money is a blessing from God. Life cannot go on without money. Jobs and business development are vital to life. How we use money wisely for our good and good of others is a big question.

I had one brother who died. He did well in business, we thought. But some thought he was tight-fisted too. His first wife died and he was anxious to provide for the rainy day for the family. I had a second brother who died. Money burnt a hole in his pocket. We said he went through a fortune. He died with no money to his name but with hundreds of friends. We said it was a blessing that he never married. He might not have been able for that responsibility; so who knows?

We must learn to share, to be better persons, lovable persons. When we share, we make real friends. Time shared is more precious than money. Parents say that time is never their own. What a treasure of generosity!

So making treasure just for oneself is foolish, the Lord says. *Lk 12:13-21*

Ordinary Time Week 29: Tuesday

Michael, Vera and family were celebrating a 25th marriage anniversary and a daughter's 21st birthday. As I waited for them at the restaurant, a young waiter in his twenties welcomed me. He was bright and good-humoured, making me feel special. When I mentioned football he enthused and told me how he got a few hours free for the international game. When my friends arrived, his welcome was equally warm. I began to ask myself, 'Where did this young man get all this?' He seemed quite unaware of his liveliness, humanity and ability to make another feel good. What is the secret here?

I have come that you may have life – liveliness. How Lord? Is it education? Is it reading? Is it home? Is it the influence of friends? How do we tap-in on the other's personal mood, stand in their shoes? How can we be glad with those who are glad, sad with those who are sad?

Jesus calls us to affirm life, be alive now in this life. It is much more of the heart than of the head, I think. God Our Father putting on an apron, sitting us down at table, waiting on us. Is this crazy, or love gone crazy with generosity?

Be like men waiting... *Lk 12:35-38*

Ordinary Time Week 29: Wednesday

Life is full of waiting, waiting for children to grow, waiting for results, waiting for items for the house, waiting for change. I saw a young girl in a restaurant. She was waiting for her boyfriend. When he arrived, their faces were alight with youthfulness and joy. He took an engagement ring out of his pocket. She opened the box and fitted on the ring with delight. She rotated her finger so that the ring caught the light at different angles. She then presented him with his ring. They kissed gently. They had little or no interest in food. Just moments of shared happiness. As they left I said, 'Congratulations.' They both came back to show their rings and to tell their story.

A story of waiting in joyful hope, not boring because the meeting was enlivened with love, a love that hints at a wondrous world and a wonderful God. Our Father knows that a lot of our waiting is painful but precious. Our patience is tried. There is more to all this waiting than meets the eye. The poor woman said, 'I look forward to death. It will be my first holiday – and maybe my first engagement too.'

You too must be ready for the Son of Man is coming. *Lk 12:39-48*

Ordinary Time Week 29: Thursday

In school yesterday, Jacinta in Senior Infants was showing me her left wrist. It was heavily plastered in a kind of cement with messages written on the white surface. She had fallen and broken her left wrist. But she was very busy now using her right hand to draw and write. The teacher explained that Jacinta always used her left hand to paint and draw. She could not use her right hand. But now she had to use her right hand. It was just as good as the left.

There are secret blessings hidden in mishaps, disappointments, separations, even death. How to see them is the problem. Sometimes, looking back, we can see blessing. Most often we cannot see. Jesus was anxious to light a fire for us that would warm our heart and help us to keep trying.

I have come to bring fire – I wish it were blazing. *Lk 12:49-53*

Ordinary Time Week 29: Friday

I really love that story of The Blind Beggar, Bart. All he did was make noise, shouting. Jesus stopped to notice and call his name. Funny the people with Jesus didn't notice him and passed him by. Worse really, they told him to shut up. One can be on Jesus' team and still be blind to people. Jesus told the crowd to bring him to him. In the very action of helping the 'nobody', they changed and began to see differently. It was not 'Shut up' now, but 'Have courage!' They helped him up.

Think of all the noise-makers in our world of protests, marches, violence. Jesus shows us a way of seeing people – that is faith. Ugly nuisances, including me and you, are people precious to him, warts and all, and known by name.

How is it you do not know how to interpret these times?
Lk 12:54-59

Ordinary Time Week 29: Saturday

A young mother dies, a child is killed, a marriage is broken, a family member is in disgrace. We cry in our hearts. 'What wrong did we do? Why did this happen to us?'

Jesus says it is not because of any sin or fault that this happens. These things are not God-sent. We have to try to see God and life in a different way. Jesus invites us to change our thinking, our attitude, to God, to ourselves and to others. He calls this 'repent'. He even says that when we change attitude we bring a kind of new life to ourselves. We shake off the stranglehold of death. He invites us to see God as Father, who loves us first and always. He invites us to see ourselves as a wonder of God's goodness, accepted despite our failings and limitations. He invites us to see people as blessing and the world as God's gift.

Look here – I've been coming to look. *Lk 13:1-9*

Ordinary Time Week 30: Monday

Children give me great joy when they shake hands. There is a sensation of touch that warms the heart and wins the heart. I think that parents who encourage and love their little ones into shaking hands do a wondrous job.

Touching got Jesus into trouble. It was through touching that he re-assured people, and made them feel good despite handicaps. He told people that he loved them. He had to take on the authorities who said that touching certain people or touching certain things on the Sabbath was not right.

Sometimes I sense an unease associated with this great blessing. We don't seem to be able to talk about feelings. There is stunted growth here, which spills over sadly into friendships, marriage and indeed into the way we see God.

I remember a shattered widow saying to me years after her husband died, 'All I long for is just somebody to hold me.' I'm sure we all share that feeling, but haven't the courage to say the words. Surely there is blessing in 'the holding and being held without possessiveness.'

He laid his hands on her – a daughter.   *Lk 13:10-17*

Ordinary Time Week 30: Tuesday

We often say 'inside out'. We know someone or some place 'inside out' and 'outside in'. God tells us his presence is 'inside out' and 'outside in', it is in all of his creation. St Patrick felt surrounded by God's presence in all the happenings of his life. On the Celtic Cross, it is a presence in nooks and corners, in twists and turns, in circles and saints all interwoven. Sky and water, field and forest, family and friends are all of nature's blessings.

The Kingdom is like a mustard seed ... like yeast.   *Lk 13:18–21*

Ordinary Time Week 30: Wednesday

I asked Mary would she help us with the Envelope Collection. She said, 'I'm attending hospital at the moment, but if I get over this bout, I'll collect for you every day of the week.' I don't know if Mary is a Church-goer, but I do know she is a good family person and a prayerful person, though she would be slow to see this in herself. Our vision of what religion means can sometimes be very narrow.

Jesus was always trying to broaden our vision of God's goodness and great mercy. He is the God whose mercy rests on all he made. Mary's sickness, wishes, and longings are all related to prayer. St. Paul sees all human desires being carried by the Spirit of God and expressed for us to our Father, because, he says. 'We are not able to find the words. He is always living to make intercession for us.'

Sir, will only a few be saved? *Lk 13:20-30*

Ordinary Time Week 30: Thursday

We all like to get together with our friends. We gather for all kinds of occasions and celebrations. We are invited to gather together in the presence of God because it is good for us and helps community. Jesus presents himself as the one who gathers us.

A woman coming out of a store lets her beautiful vase fall. A student passing-by picks up the broken pieces, opens her handbag and produces a wonder glue. She pieces together the scattered parts. 'How odd that a passer-by should have glue in her bag,' someone remarked.

How wonderful that someone should have such thought and kindness in gathering together broken pieces of life.

How often have I hoped to gather your children. *Lk 13:31-35*

Ordinary Time Week 30: Friday

A little boy was visiting a big cathedral. The little boy was fascinated by the stained-glass windows with all kinds of people shining in painted styles. He inquired, 'What are the bright people in the windows?' Dad said, 'They are the saints.' The little boy inquired further, 'What are saints?' While Dad was fishing for an answer, the little boy said, 'I know what saints are! They are people that let the light shine through them.'

The light that shines through the saints is called kindness and sharing, caring and bearing with others. This kind of light shines through us every day when we care for family, prepare meals, do the work, think of a neighbour, pray for a friend, be happy for those celebrating. The best light is not the one we throw in the sky that makes a bang or a colour. A better light is a gift to the poor, an offering to Vincent De Paul, a thought that calms a fear.

Which of you if his son falls into a well will not pull him out?
Lk 14:1-6

Ordinary Time Week 30: Saturday

One person who stands out in my heart and memory from boyhood days is Jimmy the postman. He encouraged me and taught me to play football and would get me football boots on loan. I never heard a rough word from his mouth and he always believed in playing the ball when others would try to settle parish rivalries on the field. He got a few of us on the county team and it was a taste of Paradise to be a local hero. He brought unique distinction to the parish when we won a county Minor Final at a time when winning was unheard of in our town. I cherish the medal that I got that day.

He asked me to come to his funeral with a prayer. For me he was the humble exalted and the exalted in humbleness.

The man who humbles himself will be exalted. *Lk 14:1-7-11*

Ordinary Time Week 31: Monday

Sheila Cassidy tells about two patients terminally ill with cancer. One was a gracious and generous woman, grateful for kindness. She related well to nurses and doctors, and was befriended by family and visitors. The second patient was not pleasant. She was a prostitute. Her man had left her for a younger woman. Her daughter had left her to go on the street. She never had a real friend and now she was bitter and rude, shouting insults in her pain and agony. She had a sense of humour. She was not able to pay back the courtesies, greetings, pleasantries that life expects. Maybe if she was ever loved for her own sake, the story would be different. People that cannot pay back, Jesus says are real blessings for us and indeed for themselves. Countries that can't pay back are good for us too and are blessed in their way. This is not a language of bank or business but a language of love and lavish generosity – God's language.

They cannot pay you back. You are fortunate. *Lk 14:12-14*

Ordinary Time Week 31: Tuesday

They hang around in dark corners behind the shops. My mother would call them corner boys. Now they are called gurriers and cider-drinkers. They skip school regularly. Matt and Rita like them. Rita invited the leader to come to a meeting at the Community Centre to discuss what they would like us to do for them. 'We would welcome your suggestions,' she said. Six arrived for the meeting. To get the discussion-ball rolling Matt asked, 'Why have you come here to-night?' The leader said, 'Because it is warmer here than outside.' They got free football and film-viewing in warm surroundings for over an hour. Their eyes were full of surprise and appreciation for this kindness. 'We're going to organise some way to involve them with minimal charge,' Matt said. Maybe we have to put up with graffitti and messing from kids who want to make a name or be noticed. But really they need our help most.

Go out quickly into the streets and alleys of the town, bring in the poor, crippled and lame. *Lk 14:15-24*

Ordinary Time Week 31: Wednesday

Somebody said that there is a world of difference between reading about love and being-in-love. People described on radio recently what being in love is like – one sees the other person differently, making sacrifices becomes joy. We are taken out of ourselves in care and concern.

There is a great difference between knowing things about Jesus and seeing life in a Jesus-way. Jesus calls it 'following me'. He says, 'Seeing-the-Jesus-way involves relating to father, mother, brother, sister, wife, children.' It is concern about oneself. It includes the world of business and the world of politics. It is about attitudes to everyday life. It includes all the activities of the day. God is not on the sideline of life. He is on the playing pitch.

Our few morning prayers help our vision for the day and renew our heart to cope with self and others.

Now great multitudes went to him. *Lk 14:25-33*

Ordinary Time Week 31: Thursday

The religion and the God that has time for the stray dog, the lame duck, gladdens the heart. Somehow, if religion or rules restrict God's mercy, limit his lavish generosity or present him as small minded, people shy away. His mercy rests on all that is. I sometimes feel that in the Sacrament of Forgiveness a new joy, new life has to be found.

I often thought that is was a bit unfair 'fussing over the one lost sheep (probably lost through his own stupidity) while forgetting the 99 goodies, until I noticed the words *repent* and *joy* refer to the one lost, not the 99 virtuous. I sense the Lord's humour. There is no such thing as 99 virtuous. The so-called virtuous had the wrong angle on God. 'Repent' means getting a right angle on God, realising that he is all-loving Father and Mother. We cannot earn or merit his love. We are wonders of his making, loved not because we're perfect, but in our weakness, limitations, and endless failings.

The lost sheep has the right angle. There is rejoicing over one repentant sinner. *Lk 15:1-10*

Ordinary Time Week 31: Friday

We can waste money and waste time. A lot depends on the way we waste. Some say that God our Father wastes extravagantly his blessings on us. There is indeed over-abundance in his generosity, and the Jesus celebrations weren't lacking in an overflow. 'Bring them in from the highways and byeways', and the left-overs after feeding five thousand filled twelve baskets – what kind of waste is this? Mary wasted perfume on Jesus. It was a sign of her love for him and some say gave him strength and courage to face his ordeal. So wasting for love's sake is admirable.

I saw a father wasting time today with his little girl in the Park. He gave her a swing on a low branch. They strolled through the leaves. They looked at the ducks in the pond. This time wasted was real love and a gift that cannot be substituted for by a wrapped gift.Wasting time on oneself is important too in coping with the work of life. Wasting time on God is prayer. Wasting money on flowers and gifts, calls and visits make life good. The unjust steward's waste seems a total self-interest, a fiddle for himself. Jesus says it is not the way to become fully human.

A Steward denounced for being wasteful. *Lk 16:1-8*

Ordinary Time Week 31: Saturday

'There is a lot of rubbish talked about money,' the young man said. Money is a basic necessity of life. It is the price of survival. It is our daily bread. People who are talented with money are invited to use money wisely to make a better world, to make employment, to create business opportunities - to be stewards of our world and help the less fortunate people. We have a Christian obligation to make money work for our good and the glory of God's kingdom.

The Lord never canonised poverty. He spoke frequently against it, because it can de-humanise people. He encouraged us to be realistic about poverty of spirit. We are always dependent, weak people in need in all kinds of ways. We cannot give ourselves a breath, a sunrise, a sunset. We cannot buy love or frienship. All is given.

Use money to win friends. *Lk 16:9-15*

Ordinary Time Week 32: Monday

A man said that he had no problem loving his brother who lives five thousand miles away. It was the people at home that he found difficult. Our daily obstacles are the people who live with us and surround our lives everyday. A neighbour's dog barking day and night, children involved in squabbles, boasting, jealousy. I admire people who are good at talking things out, rather than talking behind backs. Being humble or realistic enough to say, 'This annoys, irritates. I know it is not intended.' This is peace-making language. A blessing.

Reprieve him ... Forgive. *Lk 17:1-6*

Ordinary Time Week 32: Tuesday

'He never forgot the run of himself.' I've often heard people say these words. 'She has forgotten the run of herself, with airs and graces.' I guess what people mean is that we're forgetting home, background, origins, forgetting to be ourselves. Sheila Cassidy tells of her restless struggle to find her niche in life. She went to a monastery. The Abbess said, 'Why don't you try to be Sheila for a change?'

In golf they say you have to get the stance right in order to play well. Our stance is we are not self-made, we are of God. We don't have to force God to love us. He is love. In him we live, move and have our being. The God we meet everyday is in the learning to be ourselves and love ourselves as we are, and in allowing others to be themselves and learning to love them as they are. We are surely ambassadors rather than overlords.

We are merely servants. *Lk 17:7-10*

Ordinary Time Week 32: Wednesday

John died in his late 70s. Maisie did her best, caring for him. She told me that she prayed through Padre Pio for three requests: that he wouldn't have much pain, that it wouldn't be too prolonged and that he would go to Blanchardstown Hospital before the Hospice. He did not like the thought of the Hospice. A friend helped her with number three. But all requests were granted.

What I like about that little story is the desire people have to be intimate with God. We want to think of God as close, as friend. That's what Christ means. Often we use different symbols to express this closeness.

There is also a healing in this praying. Healing goes on all the time, most often through neighbours and ordinary people in our lives. Nine of ten lepers were cured but only one was healed – the one who came back to give praise.

One has come back to give praise. *Lk 17:11-19*

Ordinary Time Week 32: Thursday

Charlie said a few words from his new self-drive wheelchair, 'I would not be here to-night only for my wife Mary, my daughter Joan and loyal friends. I have had ten operations in two years in hospital, and lost two legs. I want to thank you for this mobile wheelchair – all who organised and contributed. I can now visit a neighbour, go for 'a stroll', take the fresh air.' The people in the lounge were led in song by a solo guitarist celebrating Charlie's new life. On stage beside the guitarist was a local man with Downs Syndrome. He imagined he was a drummer. He went through fantastic movements, gyrations and rythms. The sweat poured from him. Someone said, 'He enjoys that better than if he could really play.' Nobody in the audience was surprised or amused because he is always part of the furniture and accepted there. He belonged. The guitarist thanked the audience and he said, 'I want to thank my side-kick here, Drummer Dooley.' Dooley's night was made too. He was in an ecstasy of joy. God in hidden places indeed.

You must know the Kingdom of God is among us. *Lk 17:20-25*

Ordinary Time Week 32: Friday

We hear a lot about self-development to-day. There are all kinds of courses – exercise therapy, retreats and pray-ins. The writer asked, 'Can we ever find a centre in ourselves that is free from struggle, the constraints of life and the demands of others?' Finding oneself is always related to others and can't be done alone.

The three persons of God are for each other. Real freedom can only be 'for' not just 'from'. Jesus was free, but had to bear the brunt of people and even death.

Anyone who loses life in the demands of husband, wife and others, selling, planting, building keeps it safe. *Lk 17:26-37*

Ordinary Time Week 33: Monday

It is how we see things that is important, Jesus says. He is continually inviting us to look at life this way: God is Father and Mother to us. We are all precious, loved with all our limitations. The ordinary world is full of God's presence. How we look at things can change our whole life.

You can see this in the story of the poor, blind beggar. The people ignored him or told him to be quiet till Jesus turned and paid him special personal attention. As soon as he took this positive approach to what the people saw as a non-entity and a nuisance, they all changed! They became kindly and encouraging. 'Have courage! He is calling you!' they said.

It is how we see things that is important.

The people in front scolded him. *Lk 18: 35-43*

Ordinary Time Week 33: Tuesday

There is eating and drinking in the story of Zacchaeus. It is a story about wanting to see, wanting to see more in ourselves, in others and in the world. Despite his wealth and his unpopularity, Zacchaeus was anxious to see. He made his move and Jesus looked at him. Jesus then asked him for a favour, which is a gracious way of saying, 'I need you. You belong.' Zacchaeus jumped down and welcomed Jesus joyfully into his home. We love to be asked – but it is up to us to respond.

The begrudgers were there too. Their version was full of complaint and criticism of sinners. Jesus struggles to change our views of people and of life. He is always inviting us to openness.

For the Son of Man comes to seek and save what was lost.
Lk 19:1-10

Ordinary Time Week 33: Wednesday

I sometimes get letters which irritate me. When you think you're doing your best, it irks to read criticism. Then you can wallow in your annoyance, and even respond in like manner, or you can try to change the attitude which leads you to being annoyed in the first place. Nothing is good or bad, it has been said, but thinking makes it so.

The Lord is always inviting us to this therapy of changing our attitudes and freeing ourselves to grow more human. The servants hated their king and so one of them made nothing of the pound he was given.

We need help to see ourselves and our neighbours in the way God sees us. All prayer is about this openness.

His compatriots hated him. *Lk 19:11-28*

Ordinary Time Week 33: Thursday

The caller spoke about her abortion. She was a victim. It had to be this way. She felt dreadul – angry with herself, angry with humanity, angry with Church and State. Another caller wished to comfort and heal this broken spirit. I wondered how?

Jesus says that there is peace, but that it is hidden from our eyes. There is compassion in the hiddenness, as if to say that the peace is there for us, but it will not be forced upon us.

In spite of all our meanness, we have enormous capacity for forgiveness, and to forgive self. To forgive is like deciding to light a candle rather than curse the darkness, to begin on the road to peace and harmony.

If you... only understood... the message of peace...   *Lk 19:41–44*

Ordinary Time Week 33: Friday

The church at Ballymore Eustace was rebuilt after a fire. At the opening, Archbishop Connell said that God does not need a church to live in, but we need a church to remind us of God's presence throughout our world, in the bits and pieces of our everyday lives.

He is present in the face of every flower, in every cloud that scurries by and in every sunrise and every sunset. His most hidden and obvious presence is in the ordinariness of ourselves – being who we are, and accepting our neighbours as they are. The house of God helps us to see again and again with fresh eyes and celebrate.

My house will be a house of prayer. *Lk 19:45-48*

Ordinary Time Week 33: Saturday

President de Gaulle had a mentally retarded daughter. When the child died, de Gaulle comforted his wife at the graveside and said, 'Don't weep for Anne. Now she is like any other child.'

Luke Kelly had a song about a retarded child which went, 'Scorn not his simplicity but try to love him all the more.'

Jesus did not get involved in obscure arguments about the life hereafter. His good news was about living life now, in the love of God and of the neighbour. He would say that we have a million ways of being life-giving to each other – a word of encouragement, an offer to mind the baby and give the mother a break, sharing a joy, a listening heart. Or just being present in prayer.

To God all are in fact alive. *Lk 20:27-40*

Ordinary Time Week 34: Monday

'When is the Holy Spirit present?' The Confirmation Class had to write down six 'whens' and there would be three small prizes. But I decided to put all the efforts into a bag and select by Lucky Dip instead of selecting the cleverest. Our world likes stars, performers and success.

Jesus asks us to look again at other 'whens' and see more than star appearances: a mother walking to the shop with the children, a father taking his child on a bus trip, nurses trying to humour pained and frightened people. Many people have to cope with alcoholism, gambling, separation, death and a mass of other disappointments and stresses, none of which are recorded in any Book of Special Achiements.

Jesus says, 'Notice that widow, She has put more generosity into living than many of those who steal the headlines.'

He happened to notice a poor stricken widow. *Lk 21: 1-4*

Ordinary Time Week 34: Tuesday

When the people praised the magnificent splendour of the Temple, they did it in the presence of the one who was the Temple, sent by God to gather his people. There was much more to this Temple than splendid walls, golden tabernacle and fine stonework. He lived life to the full as a human person, and he speaks like a mother to us: 'Take care. Don't be frightened. Live the day that God has sent, rubbing shoulders with all those around you, meeting the setbacks and disappointments that come up, because I am with you. You are my people, my friends, my temple.'

When some were talking about the Temple ... *Lk 21: 5-11*

Ordinary Time Week 34: Wednesday

'The writing is on the wall,' is a phrase we've all heard often. It could refer to an exam, a football match, a sickness or a tragedy. Only today I learned where it came from. The king was having a whale of a time with wine, women and song, and then a hand appeared writing on the wall. Daniel then interpreted the hand and told the king that his life-style wouldn't work because he was trying to play God and had forgotten God's blessings.

Jesus was seen as another Daniel who interprets life for us and promises to be with us, even in the darkest hours. The God of Jesus Christ is the God of strength and might, but also the God of weakness and compassion. He will be with us if we trust. There is always hope.

I myself shall give you wisdom. *Lk 21: 12-19*

Ordinary Time Week 34: Thursday

A friend of mine doesn't like the phrase, 'born-again Christian' be-cause it implies that only some people have the Holy Spirit in their pocket. They 'see the light' and there is a danger that they might become some sort of elite.

There are many things that we don't understand, but, if we get the picture of God as anything other than a loving, caring, forgiving Father, then we can be sure that we are misunderstanding again. It is safer to stick to a few balanced basics. We are loved into life, not because we're good – not to mention perfect – and not because of anything we have achieved, but because God is love. We cannot buy or merit God's love; it is given because he wants us to share it with him. If we can learn to see this as Jesus did, God's love will spill out through us in all our actions in everyday life and in all creation.

When these things begin ... your liberation is near at hand.
Lk 21: 20-28

Ordinary Time Week 34: Friday

The kingdom of God is referred to often in the Bible and in our re-ligion. It means 'God's Rule', 'God's presence'.

A young girl saw a dog knocked down by a passing car. She took the dog home, rang the Vet and called the Dogs' Home. The Vet said it was kindest to have the dog put down, so she waited there till it was all over. Then she went out round the doors to try to find the owner, but without success. A few days later, the owner ar-rived to her house with a thank-you card and a box of chocolates.

Wherever there is life, there is God's kingdom. Whenever one has compassion for the pains and worries of another, God's kingdom is there. Whenever one says 'Thanks', there is God's kingdom.

When you see these things, know that the kingdom of God is near.
Lk 21: 29-33

Ordinary Time Week 34: Saturday

The trees look naked and bereaved today. The family of leaves has gone away, has flown the nest. There is great beauty in all this vulnerability, just one more showing of the love and majesty of God through his creation. And it is from the same God that we get the gift of seeing and appreciating his loving presence all around us.

Praying is waiting on God, noticing and celebrating his presence all around us. It is a gift which refreshes the human spirit and beckons us towards the wondrous life in the arms of our loving Father and Mother.

Stay awake ... praying at all times. *Lk 21: 34-36*

First Monday of Advent

'Say a prayer. I'm going to hospital today for a test.'

We can be paralysed with fear and anxiety, depression and disappointment. God does come to heal us through the hearts, minds, smiles and courtesies of people around us – the personal touch.

There are rarely cures, but there is plenty of healing. We have the power to heal with words, listening and empathy.

'My servant is paralysed and in pain.'
'I will come and cure him.'   Mt 8:5-11

First Tuesday of Advent

An artist asked me to look at the mountains in Connemara. 'How many colours can you see?' he asked. I had never noticed such variety of colours and changing shades before .

Insight is a gift of wisdom:
insight into one's own special creation,
insight into other people,
insight into our world - God's copybook.
Jesus brings this insight.
Lord, fill my mind with your light.

Happy the eyes that see what you see. Lk 10:21-24

First Wednesday of Advent

A young man was angry with God because of all the famine and hunger in the world. That night he had a dream. God spoke to him and said, 'I have done great things for the poor and hungry.' The young man said, 'Like what?' God said, 'I sent you.'

A little hungry boy said, 'God sent big people to us to share food, but they forget.'

I do not want to send them off hungry. Mt 15:29-37

First Thursday of Advent

A friend of mine, and a great community person, had his own description of a Christian in a parish. 'Is the person prepared to knock at doors and sell tickets?' was his test. 'We don't like asking. We don't like asking for money. We don't like asking for others.'

There is a variety of gifts and talents. The Lord does put stress on the helping hand and he did say, 'Ask'.

It is not those who say 'Lord, Lord' who will enter the Kingdom of Heaven, but the person who does the will of my Father.
Mt 7:21, 24-27

First Friday of Advent

One line I can remember from a retreat was very powerful. 'Your weakness is your passport to heaven.' I thought that my prayers and my good deeds would be heavenly cash. Now I think St Paul was right when he said, 'It is not for anything we did that God loves us. It is his own loving kindness.' We are loved in weakness, warts and all.

Faith is really trying to believe this unconditional love. God makes all the first moves. Jesus was helpless with those who thought they did no wrong, the so-called virtuous and those who had all the answers. Life is a great and beautiful mystery, full of greys, and no two human beings are the same. Somehow we have to be honest, admitting we don't see and we don't hear.

... and their sight returned. *Mt 9:27*

First Saturday of Advent

A spiritual writer was explaining that the secret that Jesus had with his people was that he made them feel good. He said 'He empowered people.' Each person is a unique expression of God's love with mysterious dignity. For a people crushed by all kinds of inhuman rules and regulations of State and religious groups, the word of Jesus was a powerful life-giving force. We catch his words to people: 'Stand up! Stretch out! Go home!' He gives us his power to help others to stand, to grow in confidence, and to make a better world.

Go. Care for the Sick. Raise the Dead. *Mt 10:6-8*

Second Monday of Advent

Some people thought that a cup of tea after Mass was a bit artificial and a distraction. We are people of different moods and shades. It is no harm to remind ourselves that Mass and Sacraments are about friendship and being in touch with each other in God our Father. Look at all the people involved in the healing of the paralysed man. The children in school saw that the helpers did not give up, but made a hole in the roof, and Jesus seeing their faith ...

Enthusiasm, in young or old, is grace in action.

They lowered him on his stretcher. Seeing their faith, Jesus said ...
Lk 5:17-26

Second Tuesday of Advent

'Stray' is a word I like. One can go astray, be led astray, pick up a stray. Many a stray dog becomes a best friend. It was the good God that made 'the stray' important and indeed attractive. There is no such thing as a non-straying sheep. We're all strays, if we're honest. An old 'wino' used to say to me, 'If we didn't get in trouble, it is because we didn't get the chance.'

Jesus comes for the stray. He gathers his strays. He holds them to his heart. He leads them to their pasture.

Will he not go in search of the stray? *Mt 18:12-14*

Second Wednesday of Advent

I often wonder why wise people say, 'Don't take yourself too seriously. For God's sake relax and have a laugh.' I've a priest friend who never fails to make me laugh. What a gift he has for others!

I can see reason in to-day's Mass for not taking oneself too seriously. God says the stars were there waiting for us. Mother earth and the air we breathe were there waiting for you and me. Don't behave as if you held up the world. Learn from the eagle, training her little one to fly. She drops her and then catches her in powerful wings.

He does not treat us according to our sins.

Come to me you who are overburdened and I will give you rest.

Mt 11:28-30

Second Thursday of Advent

Have you ever noticed a little child with its parent at a busy pedestrian crossing? The little child's hand is firmly grasped by the parent, while the little one hops and dances carefree, with the free hand doing its own thing.

'I am holding you by the right hand.' He does so, not to tie us up but to make us free.

I am holding you by the right hand. *Is 41:13-20*

Second Friday of Advent

Isn't 'fed up' a funny expression? It means to be browned off, bored, not at ease. 'Fed-up' suggests 'Too much', 'Full up', 'Fed up to the gills.'

Sinead O'Connor, the singer, gets angry with music money-makers. She says that they feed young people with the wrong stuff. They tell the kids that if they are full with money, possessions and fame they will be happy. This is a lie.

One way to work off the 'fed-up' flab is to think of others and to do for others.

I, the Lord, teach you what is good for you. *Is 48:17-19*

Second Saturday of Advent

Not all homes are fully happy at Christmas. Some of the family may have dropped out from Church and their parents feel that they have failed their children, that they have lost out on important values and wise direction which would have helped them to live life well.

It is good to remember that God reaches all hearts, not always in our ways, but in his ways. To be human is to be limited and our best efforts for each other and for our families can often be frustrated. We cannot force faith on people. That is in the providence of God. The good Lord promises to be with us in our times of trouble. He identifed with poor Elijah and the troubles he had in teaching God's message. Ultimately, of course, Jesus also suffered severely himself, but he came through the darkness into resurrection.

Our prayers and wishes for family and friends always register with God. I like to say the Hail Mary, because Mary does the praying for us and, I believe, with telling effect in ways we never know.

And the Son of Man will suffer similarily. *Mt 17:10-13*

Note to Reader

Whenever December 18th falls, turn ahead to the thoughts for that day on page 152 and continue till the end of the year.

Third Monday of Advent

When questioned if he believed in the next life, the young man said, 'The more important question is, 'Do we believe in this life?' St Teresa of Avila said, 'We can't know what loving God is like, but we can have a good idea about what loving a fellow person is like.' 'There is no pie in the sky that isn't cooked on earth' means that we are blessed by God with his gifts to make a better world for ourselves, for others and for the environment. St Francis of Assissi saw God in all creation, and so did St Patrick.

Jesus had gone into the Temple and was teaching. *Mt 21:23-37*

Third Tuesday of Advent

Nancy was a newcomer to the parish. She made herself go to the Station Mass, the neighbourly get-together. It was formal and predictable, but with no 'fall -out' of friendship. She called in friendship to others, but there was no reciprocation. She stopped going to the Station Mass.

We all go through the motions of saying 'Yes' while in our hearts we mean 'No'. Sham, pretence is not good for humans, and God doesn't like it either. Window-dressing is not a substitute for hospitality.

'I will not go', but afterwards he thought better and went. *Mt 21:28-32*

Third Wednesday of Advent

Is home a place to sleep in or a place to live in? Living depends a lot on how we get on with others. This is a great challenge. Jesus was always helping people to relate together, to get on together, to be in touch. How often he says, 'Go home now.'

In the sacraments, we try to continue the work of Jesus in helping us to get on together. There is no perfection in life. Most often the only person we can change is ourselves. Communion with the Risen Lord and with his people, our neighbours, should encourage us all in our search for improvement.

Go back and tell John what you have seen and heard. *Lk 7:19-23*

Third Thursday of Advent

Maggie is almost blind, has no family or possessions, and is totally dependent on the good people who care for her in a hospital for mildly mentally-handicapped women. She is the happiest person I know. She laughs long and heartily from Monday morning to Sunday night. She is forever thankful, witty, and affectionate.

It makes me ask which is the 'real world' – Maggie's or mine? It reminds me, too, that sometimes God can transform our saddest experience of failure, separation or death and bring new life.

The Lord changed my mourning into dancing. *Ps 29*

Third Friday of Advent

All humanity is the Body of Christ. Jesus has a special eye for the outsider. A David, a Joseph, a Mary, a Peter, a Prodigal, a Widow, a Tax Collector, a Soldier, a Thief.

These are his Temple. He asks us to remember this at Christmas. Have a care for justice. Act with integrity. *Is 56:1-3*

Third Saturday of Advent

There are no perfect families. There are rifts and differences and disagreements in life. St Matthew tells us about Jesus's family – his ancestors. It is a long list but there were some very naughty people in his family blood. Yet Jesus took that blood in his veins and heart through Mary and he redeemed it on Calvary.

He does give us the power to forgive the bad blood in ourselves and in others - even real injustices that were done. He give us the strength to make the first move – a card, a phone call, a word. 'I didn't really mean it that way. I see it differently now.'

The genealogy of Jesus Christ, Son of David, Son of Abraham. *Mt 1:1-17*

December 18

A little girl asked me in school why the Angelus Bell rang twice everyday. While I was thinking, another girl chirped in, 'I know. It was like this: the angel came to Mary and said God would like you to have a baby. That was at 12 o'clock. Think about it and I'll be back for the answer at 6 o'clock.'

It makes me think Mary is not a pie-in-the-sky person but very real, a practical and earthy woman who had to cope with a child unexpectedly, a husband, relations and authorities pushing her around. Mary makes the 'ordinary' grace-filled and extraordinary.

The angel of the Lord appeared. *Mt 18-24*

December 19

Christmas week reminds us of three babies: Samson, John and Jesus. All were unexpected. The timing seemed wrong. There was awkwardness and frustration. That is the way with birth, children and life. They don't come in neat parcels. There are struggles, disappointments and conflicts in growing up in home life. We cannot see or predict the end of the line.

God re-assures us that he loves us and our world in its struggle. He helps us not so much to avoid set-backs and anxiety, but to help us through the crisis of the moment.

Elizabeth was barren. *Lk 1:5-25*

December 20

He said to her, 'Rejoice'. Sometimes I get a greeting card from a school child saying, 'I love you'. The very words make one feel good. I keep the card on the mantlepiece. God's first word to Mary was a compliment. 'Rejoice, little one, you are special, precious'. Think of all the blessings that followed from that greeting.

It is true that, if we feel loved, we want to share our love our joy with others. We want to tell. The load is easier that day.

Mary asked hereself what this greeting could mean. *Lk 1:26-38*

December 21

A little boy was afraid to sleep in the dark. His mother reassured him that God our Father was caring for him even in the dark. The little boy said, 'I know, but I'd like to touch his face.'

God presents himself with the face of a young lover, pursuing his loved one, you and me, waiting outside the house, looking up at the window for his loved one to appear, and saying, 'Your voice is sweet, your face is beautiful.'

We are God's voice and God's face to others too, because the glory of God shone on the face of Jesus Christ.

My beloved lifts up his voice and says to me
Come then, my lovely one, show me your face. *Song 28:14*

December 22

The child, from earliest days, is a never-ending topic of interest on radio chat-shows, magazines and articles. New insights, new ideas on how to develop the emerging personality abound. A good self image, a wholesome self-love seems to be the bottom line.

I associate Mary, mother of Jesus, with that good wholesome self-image. She was able to see her blessings as given. She was self confident, saying all generations would praise her. If the annunciation assured her of being loved she was quickly on her way to spread love and joy to Elizabeth. New birth, new life was on the way.

He that is mighty has done great things for me. All generations will call me blessed. *Lk 46:56*

December 23

The medical superintendent presented a gift to the hospital telephonist on her retirement. He said most often the first contact with any hospital is with the telephonist. She is truly an ambassador for the hospital. I would also add that she is also God's ambassador to the wearied, the anxious, the inquiring and the inquisitive.

One can appreciate how the word, the voice, the comment can carry messages of comfort, peace, joy, consolation. These are blessings of God's Spirit.

His power of speech returned. *Lk 1:57-66*

December 24

A little boy was busy drawing. He told his mother that he was drawing a picture of God. The mother said, 'You cannot draw a picture of God. Nobody knows what God is like.' The little boy said, 'They will know what he is like when I'm finished.'

When Jesus Christ took on a human face and a human voice, God told us what he is like.

The tender mercy of our God to visit us. *Lk 1:67-79*

Christmas Day

Bobby had a beautiful head, attractive face, but sad eyes. He sat outside the house all day, waiting for his owners to return. I tried to befriend him but he was afraid and always cowered away. Eventually, I coaxed him to take little bits of food. He would stretch forward his mouth and lick the food from the tip of my fingers, but even the slightest move of my hand to pat his head sent him fearfully away. Touching his head was a no-go area. I wondered what dreadful experiences he had of beatings on the head. Then one day I was in Bobby's house. There were friends there that Bobby knew. To my surprise and delight he let me pat him on the head, but only when he was in the company of friends. I reached him through their love and trust.

I see myself and, indeed, poor humanity in Bobby – afraid to be touched, yet longing to be loved by God our Father. The only way God can touch us, pat us on the head, is through other human touches from those who accept us as we are, and don't expect perfection. This is what God has done for us through the hands and touch of Jesus Christ. Christmas means that the 'Bobbies' need fear no more. He understands.

Do not be afraid – listen. *Lk 2:1-14*

26 December St Stephen's Day

A little girl went with her Grandpa to visit The Crib at Christmas time. When she returned home her mother inquired 'Did you see Holy God in the Church.' The little girl said, 'No.' 'But I did see his Mammy.' 'And what was his Mammy doing.' The little girl replied, 'She was cleaning and tidying at the back of the Church.'

There is a mighty lot of practical love in cleaning and tidying, preparing meals, thinking of others, offering help, especially at Christmas time.

The innocence of a child captures the real woman that is Mary. She prays for us now when we don't know what to say ourselves, and at the hour of our death.

What you say will be given to you. *Mt 10:17–22*

27 December

Christmas Eve was cold and windy. The birds were famished and hungry. They flapped against the window light looking for shelter. The man of the house opened the door and offered food but they were too frightened to approach. He opened the door of an outhouse, put on the light and left food, but the birds were scared. He was very upset. He thought to himself that the only way he could help the wee birds was to become a bird himself and then he would be able to take away their fear. At that moment, the church bell rang for Midnight Mass. The meaning of Christmas dawned on him for the first time. Jesus did become human, one of us, and how often He said to the weak and poor, 'Don't be afraid. I am with you.'

Something we have touched with our hands, The Lord who is life. *1 John 1:1-4*

28 December

A little boy spilt ink on his mother's best table cloth. An artist came by one day and he saw the cloth. From that black stain he worked out a most beautiful design which became a world-famous piece of art.

Black spots, failures, tragedy become opportunities in life too. This is the powerful message of Christ. He took on our darkened, weak flesh and transformed it and us. 'O happy fall!' we sing and teach. All humanity is graced because Jesus became human. There is always hope and promise. Behind the darkest cloud awaits a glorious sunrise. Christmas is song time.

Herod was furious when he heard he was out-witted. *Mt 2:13-18*

29 December

Anne's little boy asked, 'Is Granda dead?' 'Yes, Granda is dead and he is in heaven.' 'Is Granda alive in heaven, Ma?' 'Yes, Granda is alive in heaven,' the mother said, 'God gives him a big kiss and that makes him alive in heaven.' The little boy said, 'Ma. that must be a fabulous kiss!'

The Christmas story is even more fabulous. Not only was all humanity kissed, but God came inside our skin. He took our flesh and blood and very human living. Our religion, Christianity, is earthy, flesh-and-blood, human. Help us to witness, to be truly human.

Anyone who loves his brother/sister is living in the light.
1 Jn 2:3-11

30th December

I remember a funny movie called *Parenthood*. The father has a son Kevin who lacks confidence, lags in school and is awkward with people. The father gets involved with the football team in order to get Kevin involved. He pushes him onto the team but he's a flop. The team and others get annoyed. They're losing and it's Kevin's fault. The father is going to throw in the towel when Kevin is picked for the team. Someone didn't turn up. He got the winning score. He became a hero and was lifted off the pitch. The father goes crazy, starts doing rolls on the ground, overcome with joy. He really is willing to make a fool of himself for his son's sake. He eventually refuses promotion in his job because he wants to spend time with Kevin.

That is the story of a Holy Family, life lived in struggle and effort, tension and joy. We want the best for our kids but there is exploitation. We need people who see good in us that we don't see in ourselves. We need people who love us for ourselves, not for how we benefit them.

Meantime the child grows to maturity, and he is filled with wisdom. *Lk 2:36-40*

December 31st

I remember Tony. He served in The Taverns in London. He was a people's man. 'Tonight's party is for the separated and divorced. Tomorrow night is for the singles,' he would announce with a glint in the eye and generosity in the heart. On his funeral day, his brother told about the Christmas Day he spent with Tony and his wife. He looked forward to a threesome party. When they eventually sat down to dinner that Christmas Day, there were thirty-five people at the table. Tony lived in the highways and byeways of life. He loved the people of the highways and byeways. I caught his secret, I think, when he returned from Lourdes one time. He said what he liked best in Lourdes was 'the chapel where you cannot talk.' Now Lourdes is a bustling and sound-filled place. But Tony's God was in his heart. The whole world of people and happenings was God's playing field. Tony was a centre-field man. His God had a human face, a co-suffering God.

The Word that enlightens all men was coming. *Jn 1:1-18*

Related Columba titles

150 More Stories
for Preachers and Teachers

Jack McArdle ss cc

Fr McArdle is well known throughout Ireland as a speaker and retreat director. His first collection, *150 Stories for Preachers and Teachers,* has become a bestseller and is widely used by priests and teachers who know the power of story in communicating the Christian message. In this brand new collection of original stories, Fr McArdle offers a short reflection after each story to highlight the message which he finds in the story itself.

ISBN 1 85607 056 5
96pp
£5.99

Related Columba titles

Preaching the Word

Tom Clancy

For many years now, Fr Tom Clancy, Senior Dean in St Patrick's College, Maynooth, has been writing weekly in the *Cork Examiner*, trying to link the message of the Sunday gospel with the lives and experiences of the ordinary people. This reflection on the gospel message in the light of contemporary experience is surely the basic task of every homilist and indeed of every praying Christian. Both as a resource book for homilists and a starting point for personal reflection and prayer, *Preaching the Word* will be a welcome addition to the library of every Christian.

ISBN 1 85607 029 8
224 pages
£8.99